The Complete Book of Boat Trailering

The
COMPLETE BOOK
of
BOAT TRAILERING

*A Boatman's Guide to Trailer
Selection, Use and Maintenance*

TOM BOTTOMLEY

ASSOCIATION PRESS / New York

THE COMPLETE BOOK OF BOAT TRAILERING

————————

Copyright © 1974 by Thomas Bottomley

Association Press, 291 Broadway, New York, N.Y. 10007

————————

International Standard Book Number:
0-8096-1886-9 (hardbound)
0-8096-1887-7 (paperback)
Library of Congress Catalog Card Number: 74-9622

Library of Congress Cataloging in Publication Data
Bottomley, Tom.
    The complete book of boat trailering.

    1. Boat trailers.   I. Title.
GV775.B59   629.22'6   74-9622
ISBN 0-8096-1886-9
ISBN 0-8096-1887-7 (pbk.)

PRINTED IN THE UNITED STATES OF AMERICA

Contents

Introduction

With the proper combination of boat, car, and trailer, you can extend your boating horizons from local, familiar waters to any lake, river, bay, or other suitable waterway you can reach by road—provided there's a launching ramp at the end of that road.

If you had the time and money, you could be snorkeling in the Florida Keys during one week end, cruising the Ohio River the following week end, fishing the canyon waters of Lake Powell, Utah, on the next week end, and island-hopping in the San Juans of Puget Sound the week end after that.

You could do it, too, without stops at expensive motels along the route, because your boat could double as a camping trailer. With the right galley gear aboard, and provisions, you could keep your restaurant stops to a minimum.

Note that this takes a proper combination of boat, car, and trailer. A mismatch, or an improperly set up rig, could be a menace on the highway and a nightmare at the launching ramp. The boat, of course, must be suitable for its intended use in the water and for the type of water conditions in which it normally will operate. The trailer must be strong enough to support the weight of boat, engine(s), and all gear carried in the boat; and the car must be powerful enough to handle the load of trailer and boat without undue strain.

Further, the boat should launch easily from the trailer, and winch back onto the trailer without fuss. The trailer must be adjusted so as to provide full support for the keel and power plant, and to prevent any distortion of the hull.

Weight distribution and tire pressures are critical, and must be adjusted so that the trailer tracks in a straight line behind the car, without dangerous swaying or weaving from side to side. The hitch must be strong enough for its load, and it must distribute the towing strain over as much of the car's chassis as possible.

7

The car itself may need overload springs, plus special cooling systems for the engine and the transmission. It may be that for a larger boat, a standard auto would not have the needed power and a special differential would be required. Or even a light pickup truck might be needed to handle the load.

There are many little details, as well, that add to the proper combination of boat, car, and trailer. All will be covered in this book.

Even if your local waterway satisfies your boating needs, the trailer rig provides so many bonus advantages that it still can be a worthwhile investment. Are seasonal docking fees in your area high? Your yard or driveway becomes your marina. Is off-season storage ashore expensive? Your yard or driveway is your boatyard. Are barnacles or other marine growth a problem? The fresh-water rinse you can give your boat after pulling it out eliminates the need for special bottom paint.

And should the boat, engine, radio, or any other gear need to be worked upon, you don't have to pay a serviceman to bring his tools and parts to your boat. You can take the whole rig right to him. Also, your regular schedule of routine maintenance is much easier to follow with the boat at home, on its trailer.

Boat trailering has its limitations, of course, and the most obvious is that big boats are harder to handle than little boats. When you get much beyond 25 feet in length, launching and retrieving can be a chore beyond the capabilities of the average family crew, even with a power winch on the trailer. And here, certainly, a small truck will be needed for the towing vehicle. As a result, most boats that are trailered are less than 20 feet in length.

Inboards with standard drives aren't often found on trailers, as their exposed shafts, struts, propellers and rudders are too easily damaged. Most trailerable powerboats are outboards, or inboards with stern drives.

Can sailboats be trailered? Within the size limits noted above, the answer is an emphatic Yes. Most small sailboats are centerboard types. With board retracted and the rudder removed, they launch and retrieve easily. Masts must be unstepped, of course, to make the rig ready for the road. Some cruising sailboats with retractable keels are offered as a package with a matching trailer; these are a real delight for the sailor who wants to explore new cruising areas.

Sailing catamarans, trimarans, houseboats, and other special craft also can be trailered, using trailers specially designed for the purpose. Again, size is a limitation. If the beam of the boat or the width of the trailer exceeds 8 feet, special "wide load" permits may be necessary in many states before the rig can be taken on the road.

Some houseboats are designed to be trailered, and are furnished with a matching trailer. These are particularly suited to cross-country camping/boating trips, because you have all the comforts of home right with you.

While you do save on mooring and storage fees by trailering, there are other costs to consider. The trailer itself is a major investment, and its accessories—winch, spare wheel and tire, jack or dolly wheel, light system, tie downs, hitch, and so on—add up to quite a bit. And everything you buy needs its own schedule of maintenance.

But with proper selection, use, and care your rig will give you years of trouble-free service. The flexibility of operation that boat trailering provides in itself can more than repay you for your initial investment.

The purpose of this book is: 1) to help you select the equipment that will best suit your needs, 2) show you how to use it properly and to best advantage, and 3) how to maintain it in first-class condition.

Acknowledgments

The author wishes to express his appreciation to Hal Koch, Western News Bureau manager for Chrysler Marine, for service beyond the call of duty in supplying photographs and information for this book. Clem Koehler, of Mercury Marine, also went out of his way to provide special illustrations.

Thanks also go to the Boating Industry Association for providing the material on the Trailer Manufacturer Association requirements, and to Peg and Robin Bottomley for help with the manuscript.

I. Equipment

For maximum boat-trailering pleasure, you have to start with the boat itself. Your car should get you where you want to go, and the trailer must carry the boat, but once you get out on the water, you want the craft that is best suited to your own boating needs.

Give a lot of thought to the type of boating you plan to do. Are you primarily interested in fishing? (It's an interesting note that to the all-out *fisherman,* the boat is part of his equipment: to the *boatman,* fishing is something he may or may not do, depending on circumstances.) Will the boat be used for towing water skiers? For afternoon outings on the water? For weekend cruises?

And if you're a sail enthusiast, is there a hot one-design class you want to become active in, or do you plan day sailing, or cruising?

There are boats that are particularly suited for one purpose or another, but fortunately most boats are capable of fulfilling a multitude of functions adequately, and choice more often than not is a matter of what is available from the local dealer. An understanding of basic hull forms and what they mean, however, can help prevent the disappointment of getting a thoroughly unsuitable boat.

The Boat

All boat hulls are divided into two major classifications: displacement and planing types. Displacement hulls are characterized by round bottoms (see Figure 1). These boats displace an amount of water that is equal in weight to the total weight of the boat and everything in it. They are not fast, as hull speed is a function of hull length, based on wave-making resistance. For a boat of trailerable size, the maximum speed might be five or six miles per hour. However, very little power is needed to bring a displacement-hull boat up to speed. Most sailboats are of the displacement type; so a little outboard motor of less than 15 h.p. is about the most that's needed for them. Very few modern powerboats are displacement types.

ROUND-BOTTOM BOATS

...are large displacement-type hulls and are relatively slow-moving boats. Advantages include good seaworthiness, comfort, excellent long-range cruising ability. Disadvantages include slow speed and a tendency to roll in a beam sea.

Courtesy Chrysler Marine

Figure 1

Most powerboats—and a few sailboats—have planing hulls. A planing hull presents a broad, flat bottom to the water (see Figure 2) that tends to ride up onto the surface as the boat moves forward. Naval architects call this "dynamic lift," and a

FLAT-BOTTOM BOATS

...are those such as skiffs johnboats, prams and scows. They are the simplest and most economical type of hull form. They are very fast (if you can keep them right side up and aimed in the right direction). Essentially, the flat-bottom boat has a boxy shape. It should have slight flare on the sides (to spray water aside and help keep passengers dry). It pounds badly and is very uncomfortable in rough water, but it's a very practical type in calm, protected, shallow water. Courtesy Chrysler Marine

Figure 2

good part of the hull actually becomes airborne. Theoretically, the maximum speed is limited only by the amount of power that can be applied.

For example, you could take the average 14-foot runabout and put a pair of 150 h.p. outboard motors on the transom, and easily top the 100-miles-per-hour mark—that is, if you didn't kill yourself and sink the boat. This is why manufacturers put safe-horsepower-capacity plates on their hulls. Boats that are built for such high speeds are the hydroplanes, and they are aerodynamically designed literally to "fly" level with the water with only two sponson tips and half the propeller in contact with the water (see Figure 3). This is why they're often called "three-pointers."

The average 14-foot runabout, like most small pleasure craft, is really a semi-planing boat. The flare at the bow, the V in the forward sections of the hull are compromises; they also are features of displacement hulls. They do provide stability, maneuverability, and a better ride in choppy water than the all-out hydro.

Courtesy Mercury Marine

Figure 3. Full speed ahead!

Three major hull configurations are of the semi-planing type; each has its advantages and limitations, but often the distinctions are so slight as to be all but meaningless. The forms are the standard hull modified-V, the deep-V, and the cathedral (sometimes called the gull-wing or trimaran) which is not to be confused with the trimaran sailboat hull (see Figure 4).

Any planing hull needs more power than a displacement boat of similar size to get up cruising speed, but the standard type needs less power than the deep-V. It gets up onto plane quicker, and has a higher top speed, than the deep-V boat of similar size and power. In a chop, it will pound badly; in a following sea, the wide, flat transom tends to yaw dangerously, which can lead to broaching.

The deep-V lacks initial stability. At rest and slow speeds it will rock from side to side more than the standard planing type. It needs more power to get moving, but once on plane its stability improves, and it provides the most comfortable ride of any type in rough going, on any heading.

Cathedral hulls are characterized by the trimaran-hull shape forward, although this flattens out to a normal planing bottom in the after sections on most models. Power and speed characteristics are similar to those of the standard hull, but the cathedral offers more lateral stability at rest, and a little more usable, load-bearing space up forward. Most of the so-called "bass boats" are of this type. Most of these cathedral hulls ride well when heading into a chop, but tend to roll if running broadside to the waves. The Boston whaler and others of its type show remarkable stability on all headings.

Many boats combine elements of the standard and deep-V types, so it is hard to tell just where one leaves off and the other begins. The V, for example, is flattened out considerably; the longitudinal strakes may not run all the way to the transom.

In general, the choice is just a matter of personal preference, as variations in performance can be slight in normal use. However, some generalities are possible. If you plan to do a lot of fishing or skin diving, the cathedral hull will provide the most stable platform. For operation in waters that are often rough, the deep-V will provide the softest ride, the best directional stability. For speed or towing water skiers, the standard planing hull will function best. Trailers, of course, are available for, or can be adapted to, each of these types.

Modified-V is sharp at the
bow (to reduce pounding) and
tapers back to an almost flat
bottom at the stern (for better
planing). They're more comfortable in choppy water
than flat bottoms. They are efficient, safe, and
offer a reasonable compromise between the comfort
of the deep-V and the speed of a flat bottom.

Deep-V is usually found in
pleasure craft of 8 to 30 ft.
Such a craft is soft-riding,
dry, and maintains excellent
cruising speeds when the going
gets rough. However, they are harder to push
through the water than flat or modified-V bottoms,
and therefore require larger engines. If you want
a boat for protected waters, you probably won't
need a deep-V.

Cathedral hull is basically
a deep-V in the center with
a shallow-V on either side,
forming (as seen from the bow)
two arches (hence the name) or
a shape that is also descriptively termed "gull-
winged." It tapers back to an almost flat bottom
at the stern. Popular hull sizes run from about
14 to 28 ft. and are almost always constructed
of fiberglass. Usually the riding quality of the
cathedral is dependent upon the center V. Side
V's (often called "sponsons") trap air and spray
it under the hull to provide added lift, causing
the hull to run flat and plane quickly. Advantages
are: it requires less power for a given speed;
planes easily with less power; has good stability
(especially at low speeds); holds course well in
a disturbed sea; roomy and comfortable for family
fun; available in a wide range of models.

Courtesy Chrysler Marine

Figure 4

Small single-hull and catamaran sailboats are easy to trailer, as centerboards retract and rudders swing up for launching or retrieving, and masts are easily dismounted and lashed to the boat or to a car-top carrier for the road. Some trimarans of a length suitable for trailering (less than 25 feet) may have a beam in excess of 8 feet, which is the maximum for a trailer load in most states. To haul one of these behind the car may require special "wide-load" permits and signs, and trailering may be restricted to weekdays.

Some manufacturers offer a special breed of cruising sailboat that is sold as a package with a matching trailer. This sailboat has a retractable keel, removable rudder, and outboard motor for auxiliary power, as well as rigging that folds down for on-deck storage while trailering. It also provides full cruising facilities—usually for a maximum of four persons—and behaves well under sail.

Finally, consider the size and weight of your prospective boat in relation to the trailer that will be needed, and the total load this will be for your car. Unless you plan to purchase a new car —or a truck—you are limited to what the power, age, and condition of your present car will permit you to handle. You can check with the local dealer for your make of car for the recommended load limits.

The Car

Most passenger cars built in recent years will handle light trailer loads with just the addition of a suitable hitch, and a connector to link the car's brake, turn, and tail lights to those on the trailer. However, if your boat and trailer make a fairly heavy combination, you may need a heavier, more powerful vehicle—or at least some modifications to your present car's cooling, suspension, and brake systems.

Engine power is related to the load-hauling ability of a vehicle, but car size and weight often are more important. Obviously a little Chevrolet Vega is not suitable for hauling a 25-foot cruiser over mountain roads. It would not be suitable even with a 300-h.p. engine installed in place of the standard 90-h.p. engine. Picture the car on a fairly steep launching ramp, ready to haul out its load: The transmission is shifted to low range, the engine revs up . . . and the wheels spin! There's not enough weight on the rear wheels, and there's not enough tire surface in contact with the ramp to provide traction. While rubber burns, the rig just sits there.

At highway speeds out on the road, the slightest cross wind or even unequal tire pressure would cause the trailer to yaw, and the lateral pressure at the hitch could literally throw the little car right off the road.

This is an extreme example, of course, but it does indicate that the size of the towing vehicle must be matched to the load. In the case of the 25-foot cruiser, or other loads in the range of 6,000 lbs. or more, a van, pickup truck, or utility-type station wagon such as the International Harvester would be the most suitable vehicle.

If your trailering takes you through hilly or mountainous country where long upgrades are encountered, engine overheating often is a problem. The engine and transmission both strain to maintain speed, and enough heat is generated to overload the standard cooling system—particularly if the car's air conditioner is being used.

The solution is installation of an auxiliary transmission oil cooler. These units are made up in sizes rated to match trailer loads, and they are available from auto dealers, auto supply stores, and even from Sears, Roebuck. Price should be less than $30, and if you are handy with tools you can do your own installation. It not only helps your transmission to run cooler but also, by relieving the regular radiator of the transmission cooling job, provides more cooling action for the engine itself.

SUSPENSION

The weight of the trailer load carried at the hitch should be no more than 10 per cent of the total load—5 to 7 per cent is recommended. For a light runabout, this may amount to only 75 pounds but on bigger boats it can be 600 pounds or more. Often it is necessary to beef up the rear suspension with overload springs and heavy-duty shock absorbers to help handle this extra weight.

However, these items are readily available, the cost is reasonable, and installation is no problem.

WIRING

All boat trailers require at least taillights, turn signals, stop-lights, and a license-plate light. These must be connected with the car's wiring. If the trailer has electric brakes, these too must be hooked into the car's electrical system.

All too often one sees a connector dangling at the end of frayed wiring which, in turn, is held in place by a few scraggly turns of electrician's tape. Such a hookup is bound to fail, usually at a critical time. Buy a supply of crimp-on connectors, and buy, borrow, or rent a proper crimping tool. Then you can make the necessary cuts in the car wiring, splice in the leads from the trailer plug, crimp the connectors onto the wires, and wind up with a neat, permanent, trouble-free installation. Be sure to route the wiring to where it is out of the way and protected from damage. The connector plug also should be located where it is protected from road damage, yet accessible. Trailers made by member firms of the Trailer Manufacturers Association provide color-coded wiring, as discussed in a later chapter.

MIRRORS

When being towed on trailers, most boats obstruct vision to the rear through the car's rear-view mirror. Even the small, normal side-mounted mirrors may not let you see what is directly behind your rig on the road. Therefore, you should add big, wide mirrors that mount 8 or 10 inches out from each side of the car. These fold out of the way when not in use, or are even complete-ly detachable. They are invaluable both when on the road and at the launching ramp. Some models mount alongside the wind-shield; other models mount forward on the fenders.

THE HITCH

The proper hitch is the single most critical item in matching the car to its trailer load. Perhaps at some time you have rented a U-Haul type of trailer, and the rental agent clamped a bumper hitch to the rear of your car. If you were lucky, you returned the trailer when you were through with it, and there was no damage to your bumper.

Never use a bumper hitch on the rear of your car for towing a boat trailer. It's not just because of possible damage to the bumper, either. Your boat and trailer, even if small in size, represent a considerable investment; one that you would hate to see is no longer behind you on your trip to Lake Winnipesaukee. A bumper hitch is notoriously weak, and, also, the bumper hitch puts all the trailer tongue weight right back on the bumper, the very tail end of your car. Any motion back there, up-and-down *or* side-to-side, acts just at that point, throwing the rear of the car up-and-down or side-to-side. Besides putting a lot of strain on your bumper, this makes the car difficult to handle at any but the slowest speeds. And, finally, use of a bumper hitch to tow a boat trailer on the road is illegal in most states.

Does this mean the bumper hitch should be ruled out completely? No. Not if you have a vehicle with a strong *front* bumper, such as a Travel-All-type wagon, a van, or pickup truck. Here a securely mounted front bumper hitch can be a real help. When you're ready to launch, you unhook your trailer from the rear, and hook up to the front of your vehicle. You're driving forward to back the trailer down the ramp; maneuverability is improved, and your rear wheels, which need traction, are up on the dry part of the ramp even if the front wheels are in the water.

At one time axle hitches were fairly common. These are stronger than bumper hitches and they do help reduce the effects of trailer yawing, but the stresses are transferred to the axle housing, which puts a severe strain on the rear suspension. Use of axle hitches definitely is not recommended.

We are left with the frame hitch, and this is what you should use. This type of hitch bolts directly to the car frame, so that stresses are spread fairly evenly, and its strength is ample for all conditions. For light loads, the ball-frame hitch is adequate. This is a small bolt-on unit that attaches to the center of the frame at the rear of the car. For larger loads, we must use an equalizing platform-type hitch which bolts onto frame side members at the rear of the car and helps to transfer stresses evenly from the rear to the front of the vehicle.

For either hitch, it may be necessary to drill holes in the frame for mounting bolts. Most new cars have pre-drilled holes, so all you have to do is to get the proper hitch supplied by the dealer. Be sure the hitch has holes to take the hooks of the trailer-tongue safety chains. As noted later in this chapter, trailers are classified by capacity. Be sure the ball on your trailer hitch is the correct size for your trailer class as indicated in Table I.

TABLE I

STRENGTH RATINGS for TRAILER COUPLINGS and BALLS

Trailer classification and maximum GVWR*		Class 1 not over 2,000 lbs.	Class 2 2,000- 3,500 lbs.	Class 3 3,500- 5,000 lbs.	Class 4 5,000- 10,000 lbs.
Coupling Designation		No. 1	No. 2	No. 3	No. 4
Ball Type	Minimum ball diameter	1 7/8 in.	2 in.	2 in.	Ball and bolt shall be of such size and strength as to conform to the minimum breaking strength requirements for the specific gross trailer weight.
Minimum breaking point requirements for trailer couplings and balls "Static Bench Test"	Longitudinal tension and compression	6,000 lbs.	10,500 lbs.	15,000 lbs.	3 x gross trailer weight
	Transverse thrust	2,000 lbs.	3,000 lbs.	4,000 lbs.	1 x gross trailer weight
	Vertical tension and compression	2,500 lbs.	4,500 lbs.	7,000 lbs.	1.3 x gross trailer weight

GVWR is the Gross Vehicle Weight Rating, the total combined weight of the trailer and its maximum load.

As can be seen, the minimum ball diameter for the Class 1 trailer is smaller than the minimum required for Class 2 and Class 3. Balls for Class 4 are larger in diameter. There was recently a move to adopt a Federal Highway Safety Standard which would make it mandatory to use the largest diameter ball with the hitch for the smallest-sized trailers. As a corollary, the smallest diameter balls would be used on the hitches designed to take the heaviest loads. Of course the specifications called for this smallest-size ball to be adequate in strength for the bigger trailers. With this system, it would not be possible to couple a heavy trailer to a light-duty hitch. The proposed standard was to have gone into effect in 1972, but it never got beyond the proposal stage.

As noted earlier, power alone is not needed to handle moderately heavy loads, but in some cases it *is* necessary to get as much as possible of the power available transferred to the rear wheels, both for haul-out and for on-the-road driving. This can be accomplished by a change of differential gears to provide a higher axle ratio, i.e., more turns of the drive shaft to each revolution of the rear axles. This definitely is a professional auto mechanic's job, and it is best done by the service department of the local dealer for your make of car.

The automatic transmission has been a great boon to boat trailering when it comes to hauling a rig up a steep launching ramp. Set the transmission in low range, and you can pull the loaded trailer up with little strain on engine or transmission. With a standard transmission, it's often necessary to slip the clutch to avoid stalling out; you're revving the engine faster than normal, of course, in order to provide enough power to get moving uphill. This is extremely hard on the clutch—it overheats rapidly and the clutch plates can distort so badly as to make shifting gears impossible; at the very least, plate wear is accelerated, making frequent replacement necessary if that steep ramp is the only one available. Also, some drivers find the smoke and odor of a badly overheated clutch quite upsetting.

This does not mean, however, that every standard transmission should—or can—be replaced by an automatic, or that if your car has a standard transmission you should trade the car in for one with an automatic unit. Instead, just choose your launching ramp with care, avoid slipping the clutch as much as possible, and make sure the clutch adjustment is checked frequently.

If you do much trailering, it's wise to arrange special stowage in your car—usually in the trunk of a passenger car—for tools and gear associated with the trailer. One such arrangement is shown in Figure 5. The compartment holds masking tape, spray-type lubricant, hose clamps, chains, a spotlight, flashlight, and miscellaneous small items. Below is a length of angle aluminum bolted to the trunk floor to hold a toolbox firmly against the side of the car.

Provision should be made for housing a spare trailer wheel with tire, if it is not carried on the trailer itself.

Figure 5. This permanent compartment is built into the area of the fender. A similar shelf is mounted on the opposite side of the car.

For a station wagon, van, or camper, you can make up a trailer gear box that can be placed in the vehicle whenever the trailer is in use. To discourage theft, it should be possible to lock the box itself so it can't be opened by unauthorized persons, and to lock the box to the vehicle. Be sure to lock the vehicle itself when you are going to be away from it, and keep the keys with you.

A typical frame-hitch installation is shown in the photograph sequence, Figures 6 A, B, and C. The rear of the car is elevated and securely supported. If you can run the car up on ramps, this is fine, or place jack stands under the axles. Do not try to hold up the rear of the car with a bumper jack, or even a pair of bumper jacks, for this work.

Clamp the hitch in place or have an assistant hold it, and mark location of holes for the bolts that will attach it to the frame. Once the holes are marked, they can be center-punched, then drilled. Use of the center punch keeps the drill bit centered as it starts to cut; without its use, the drill bit may wander off to one side, leaving the hole off-center. Drill first with a quarter-inch

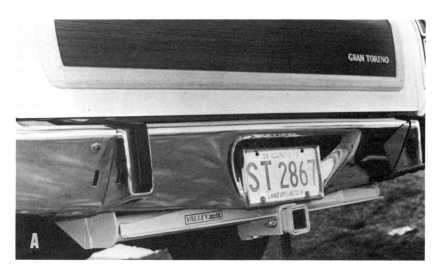

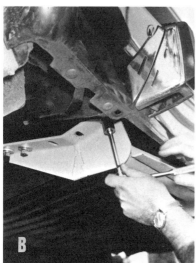

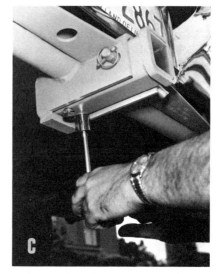

Figure 6. Installation of a frame hitch: U-bolts are inserted at the forward end of each side plate. The nuts are in place on the left-hand plate, and can be seen at the left end of that plate. Additional bolts are used to provide a more secure attachment to distribute stresses from the hitch to the car's frame.

drill, and then with a half-inch bit; this is much easier than trying to punch through with just the half-inch bit, if yours is a typical home-craftsman electric drill. With a hefty heavy-duty drill, you can start with the half-inch bit, of course.

On the hitch shown, U-bolts are inserted through from the frame at the forward end of each side plate; the nuts are in place on the left-hand plate, and can be seen at the left end of the plate, Figure 6B. Additional bolts secure the rear end of each plate. Note that this frame has a receiver tube that takes the ball assembly. The tube is bolted in place as shown in Figure 6C. All bolts must be tightened to the torque recommended by the hitch manufacturer.

On some hitches, the ball is bolted on a short length of U-shaped channel iron, which slips into a receiver tube on the hitch. The ball can be removed—to prevent theft or damage—by removing a locking pin and sliding the ball assembly out of the receiving tube.

The Trailer

Three major types of trailers are available: plain frame (see Figure 7); tilt frame (see Figure 8), and the drive-on models. Most trailers for light loads are of the plain-frame type, although plain and tilt frame trailers are available for boats of every trailerable size. The tilt frame, of course, makes it a little easier to launch and retrieve a boat without immersing too much of the trailer running gear.

Drive-on trailers have very low beds that make it possible to float the boat free when launching, and also to drive the boat into position on the trailer for haul-out. Of course the ramp angle must be fairly shallow in order to do this. Such trailers do have rollers and winches to make normal launch procedures feasible when the drive-on feature is impractical.

A trailer must be strong enough to carry the load of the boat and all its gear, plus any additional items that may be loaded in the boat when you're on the road. Also, the trailer should be long enough so that the boat doesn't overhang at the rear. Fortunately, if the trailer you select is rated to carry the proposed load, it will be long enough. Trailer manufacturers have had years of

Figure 7. Trailex aluminum trailer designed for powerboats up to 6,000 pounds. Weight is supported by rollers along keel, and multiple rollers along the chines. Use of three axles distributes the load to six wheels and tires.

Figure 8. Holsclaw tilt-frame model is for boats up to 16 feet in length, and up to 1,300 pounds weight. Note how center rollers at rear pivot to help act as guides when boat is loaded, and to give support to the transom when the boat is in position.

experience in matching weight and length characteristics, and it would be an odd boat for which a standard trailer is not available.

Figure 9. Cruising sailboat is offered as a "package" with matching trailer. Note how mast is cradled in supports near bow and transom. Fully retractable keel and detachable rudder make trailering easy, and boat can be rigged and launched by two persons in about 20 minutes. Trailer sailors must watch out for overhead wires when stepping the mast.

Member firms of the Trailer Manufacturers Association, a branch of the Boating Industry Association, have classified trailers by their capacities, in terms of the Gross Vehicle Weight Rating (GVWR). This is the combined weight of the trailer and the maximum load capacity: Class 1—not over 2,000 lbs.; Class 2—2,000 to 3,500 lbs.; Class 3—3,500 to 5,000 lbs.; and Class 4—5,000 to 10,000 lbs. Wiring, lighting, wheel and tire sizes, and in some cases brake systems, are governed by these classifications.

Each trailer carries a plate fastened to the left side of the tongue that gives the trailer capacity, along with the Gross Vehicle Weight Rating, and the maximum load to be carried by each axle, if the trailer has more than one (see Figure 10).

It is advisable to determine the maximum weight of your load by totaling the weight of the boat itself, the engine(s), fuel, water, and all gear to be carried aboard while being towed. Table II, based on one prepared by Holsclaw Bros., Inc., provides a good guide for determining total load weight. If the total comes within 100 pounds of the maximum capacity of the trailer you have selected, it is advisable to spend a little more money and get the next largest size. An overloaded trailer suspension transmits more road shock to the boat, and is subject to breakdown.

Boat support on the trailer is provided by rollers along the keel line, and rollers or padded bunkers out along the chines. The

TABLE II

FINDING TOTAL LOAD WEIGHT

ITEM	WEIGHT	ITEM	WEIGHT
Trailer max. capacity	____	spare motor	____
TOTAL (pounds)	____	food	____
BOAT AND GEAR	____	clothing	____
hull (add 20% wet wood boat)	____	marine toilet	____
motor	____	..... motorcycles at ..... lbs. ea. ...	____
battery 40 lb.	____	..... snowmobiles at ..... lbs. ea. ...	____
fuel 6.6 lb./gal. ...	____	golf cart	____
water 8.3 lb./gal. ..	____	golf clubs	____
windshield	____	miscellaneous	____
steering gear	____	TOTAL	____
tool kit, tackle box	____		
anchor, anchor line	____	How much safety margin over trailer capacity? ...	____
camp equipment	____		

MFD. BY E-Z LOADER BOAT TRAILERS
DIVISION OF JOHNSON & THIELMAN, INC.
DATE MFD.   7 / 7 3
GVWR   3 4 4 0
GAWR: FRONT   3 4 4 0   REAR
THIS VEHICLE CONFORMS TO ALL APPLICABLE FEDERAL
MOTOR VEHICLE SAFETY STANDARDS IN EFFECT ON THE
DATE OF MANUFACTURE SHOWN ABOVE.
SERIAL NO.   317796   MODEL 17SWT-2400
TYPE: BOAT TRAILER
U.S. Pat. 3,155,249 and 2,827,188   Canadian Patent 718,785

Figure 10. Trailer capacity plate gives vital statistics on trailer.

padded bunkers are a little less expensive than the rollers, but they do work well, and often the choice depends more on what is available than on any supposed advantage of one type over the other.

A bow stop is provided on the trailer to hold the bow firmly in place so that it can't swing from side to side when you are on the road. Most stops are a metal "V" with rubber pads; some are a pair of rollers mounted on a pivoted bar (see Figure 11). The frame member on which the stop is mounted can be moved forward and backward on the trailer tongue, and the stop itself often can be raised or lowered to provide the best security for the boat.

The winch, mounted above the bow stop, also may be adjustable for height. It should be about three inches above the bow eye of the boat.

Most winches on trailers of Classes 1 to 3 are manual; electric winches (see Figure 12) are desirable for loads of 5,000 lbs. or more. Electric winches also are available for smaller loads, for

Figure 11. Double roller on pivot acts as bow stop on this trailer.

those who desire this convenience. Power is supplied by the car's battery.

Manual winches are supplied with gear ratios that range from about 3:1 for light loads to 17:1 for the heaviest. The stock winch supplied with the trailer is suitable for the load capacity of the trailer, but if the ramp you normally will use is fairly steep, or if you and your crew are lightweights in the muscle department, you may want a winch with higher gearing. You'll use more turns of the winch handle to move the boat a given distance, but the turning will be easier. Fairly standard winch-gear recommendations are: 3.1 for loads to 1,500 lbs.; 6.1 for loads up to 2,600 lbs.; 12:1 for loads up to 5,000 lbs.; and 17:1 for loads of more than 5,000 lbs.

Winch lines are usually made of a synthetic fiber, such as nylon or polypropylene, or wire rope. Wire rope is strongest, of course, and should be used with loads of 5,000 lbs. or more. Nylon has greater tensile strength than polypropylene, but it does have considerable stretch. Polypropylene is usually the standard line furnished by the trailer manufacturer.

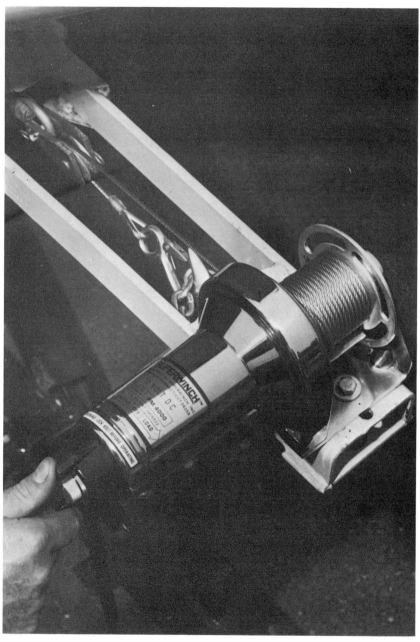

Figure 12. Electric winch by Superwinch can be used to haul boats up to 4,000 pounds onto the trailer. It is powered by the car's battery.

The number of axles provided on a trailer is directly related to load weight (each axle has two wheels, of course, one at each side of the trailer). Too much weight on a single axle could cause early failure of any component of the suspension or running gear: tires, wheels, bearings, springs, and shock absorbers.

In general, trailers for loads to 2,500 lbs. will be of the single-axle type; those for loads of more than 2,500 lbs. will have two axles. The capacity plate on the trailer tongue will indicate the load capacity (gross axle weight) of each axle in relation to the size of the wheels used on the axle. Normally, the weight is evenly distributed to each axle.

Trailer wheels usually are much smaller than those on the towing vehicle. Since your car's spare can't be used on the trailer, it's wise to get a spare wheel with the proper tire mounted on it.

There is a relation between the wheel size and the load capacity of the trailer. The larger the wheel, the greater the capacity within the physical limitations of the trailer frame. Common wheel diameters are 8 inch, 12 inch, and 13 inch. In some cases the trailer manufacturer will offer options so that the trailer can be closely matched to the proposed load.

Figure 13. Bow stop, spare wheel mount on trailer tongue, and tongue jack. Spare wheel is locked with a chain to the tongue.

Tires, of course, must be those specified for trailer use. It may be possible to fit tractor or utility vehicle tires to your trailer wheels, but these are not designed for highway use, and would be subject to a blowout at highway speeds (see Figure 14). Also, although such a tire might fit the trailer wheel rim, the tire outer

Courtesy Chrysler Marine

Figure 14. Here's the result of low tire pressure and high speed.

diameter would not match that of the trailer tire on the opposite wheel. This could cause the trailer to sway from side to side behind the towing vehicle.

Because of their small size, trailer wheels must revolve faster than those on your car to cover the same distance, and there is a tremendous heat build-up in the tire and wheel. Trailer tires are designed to withstand this heat; other tires are not.

Two types of trailer couplings are in use: one has a screw-down knob that brings the coupler lock snug under the hitch ball on the car; the other uses a lever action for the same result. There is no particular advantage of one type over the other. You get what the manufacturer has installed; he usually offers no option. The coupler will be marked with the size of the hitch ball to which it should be attached.

Every trailer should come equipped with a safety chain—two chains are preferable—that is to be attached by means of "S" hooks slipped through holes provided on the hitch. Then, if the hitch ball should break off or the coupler fail, the trailer still will be attached to the car.

Trailers with load capacities of 1,000 pounds or more should be equipped with brakes. These are a legal requirement in many states. They may be the "surge" brakes that are activated by inertia when the car's brakes are applied (see Figure 15). With these brakes there is a slight time lag, of course, but it is so slight that it does not affect the behavior of the trailer behind the car. Other trailer brakes are activated electrically when the car's

Courtesy Chrysler Marine

Figure 15. Hydraulic surge brakes feature hand lever that can be used to test brakes, or to set them when trailer is disconnected from car.

brakes are applied, so they go into action simultaneously with those on the car.

With no brakes at all, a heavy trailer would tend to push a car forward when the car's brakes are applied. In addition to increasing the distance needed for coming to a stop, this action in a turn could throw the rear of the car off the road or into oncoming traffic.

Every trailer has an electrical system for taillights, brake lights, turn-signal lights, and clearance lights. These are subject to the normal abuse of travel over the road, as well as an occasional dunking during launching or retrieval operations, so all components should be selected for this service with an eye to corrosion resistance.

Some of these light units can be detached from the trailer before it is backed into the water, and it is often possible to modify a fixed-light installation so that it can be removed. Use a strip

TABLE III

TRAILER LIGHTING EQUIPMENT
For trailers less than 80 inches wide

ITEM	LENS MARKING	LOCATION
2 Class A Stop and Turn Signal Red Lamps	S and I	On the rear, one on each side of the vertical centerline at the same level, as far apart as practicable, but no closer than 24 inches center to center.
2 Red Tail Lamps	T	
4 Red Class A Reflex Reflectors	A	On the sides, one on each side as far to the rear as practicable.
2 Red Side Marker Lamps	P1 or P2	
2 Amber Class A Reflex Reflectors	A	On the sides, one on each side as forward as practicable exclusive of the trailer tongue.
2 Amber Side Marker Lamps	P1 or P2	
License Plate Lamp	L	At the license plate to illuminate the plate from the top or sides.

of plastic electrician's tape to seal the connector plugs before backing the trailer into the water.

Table III shows the light requirements for trailers less than 80 inches in width, for certification by the Trailer Manufacturers Association. Note that both reflectors and marker lamps are specified for the sides of trailers.

Table IV shows the light and reflector requirements for trailers of 80 or more inches in width, plus optional clearance lights that can be used.

TABLE IV

TRAILER LIGHTING EQUIPMENT

Trailers of 80 or more inches in width shall be equipped as above plus:

3 Red Identification Lamps	P1 or P2	On the rear as close to the vertical centerline as practicable in a horizontal row, with lamp centers spaced between 6 to 8 inches.
2 Amber Clearance Lamps	P1 or P2	On the front to indicate the overall width of the trailer, one on each side of the vertical centerline at the same height, and as near the top as practicable
2 Red Clearance Lamps	P1 or P2	On the rear to indicate the overall width of the trailer, one on each side of the vertical centerline at the same height, and as near the top as practicable.

Optional Clearance Lamps for boat trailers only.

2 Amber/Red Clearance Lamps	P1 or P2	One on each side near the midpoint at the extreme width showing amber to front and red to rear.

Location of lights, and typical wiring layouts, are shown in Figure 16. The auxiliary circuit indicated at the car connector plug would be for electrically actuated brakes.

As shown in the illustration, the trailer frame is the ground for all trailer wiring. It is connected to the car frame through the connector plug.

NOTE: Do not rely on metal-to-metal contact of the coupler to the hitch ball to provide the ground path back to the car frame. The lubricant used on the ball will destroy the effectiveness of the ground, so that the trailer lights will not operate, or will flicker on and off.

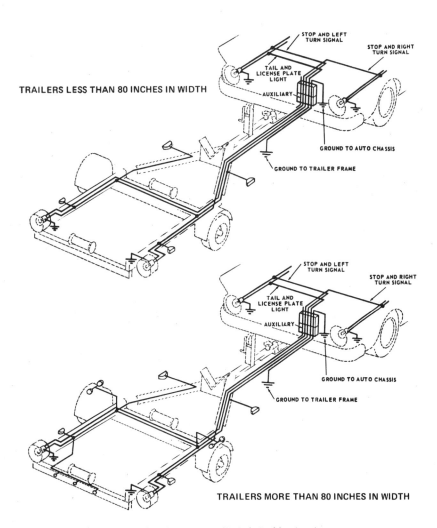

Figure 16. Location of trailer lights, along with typical wiring layouts.

Figure 17. Trailer parking jack.

Not included as standard equipment on most trailers but almost always available as an option is a trailer parking jack that can be clamped or bolted to the trailer tongue. The jack can be used to raise the tongue to the proper height for hookup to the car, and it provides a firm support for the tongue during periods of storage. Most jacks incorporate a wheel at the bottom so the trailer can be maneuvered about when it is not connected to the car (see Figure 17).

Other trailer accessories include lifting handles that attach to the tongue, for use in lifting the trailer tongue when no jack is used; spare wheel bracket, mast holders for use when a sailboat is trailered, fender step pads, and guides that attach to fenders or frame for use as aids in lining the boat up with the center of the trailer when it is being hauled out of the water.

THE USED TRAILER

A properly maintained trailer has an almost indefinite life, so it is possible to purchase a used one in good condition at a fraction of the price of a new one. And often a trailer is part of the package when buying a used boat. In either case you'll want to know if the trailer is worth the asking price, and if it is sturdy enough to carry the proposed load.

Many older trailers do not carry a capacity plate on the tongue, so how do you know if it will carry the weight of your boat and gear? Start by finding out, if possible, from the previous owner the size and type of boat the trailer carried. If this load is much lighter than yours, the trailer probably is rated for the lighter load. Look for something bigger.

Another way is to match the trailer against those shown in current trailer manufacturers' catalogs. The chances are that you'll find a cataloged model that is almost identical to the used one, and then the catalog information can be used as a guide.

Even if you are satisfied that the trailer is of ample capacity, check it when unloaded to see if the frame is straight and not twisted in any way. Sight along the line of the keel rollers to see if the rear of the trailer sags down in the area behind the axle. If so, it's an indication the trailer was too heavily loaded by the previous owner's rig. Also check cross-frames for sag in mid-section. Such sag could cause chine-line rollers or bunkers to pinch in toward the centerline, putting an unwanted stress on the bottom of the boat.

Another check you should make, with your boat or an equivalent load on the trailer, is with a long straightedge along the top of the axle. A bowed axle is another sign of an overloaded trailer. Check, too, the condition of springs and shock absorbers. It may be that the trailer is of the correct capacity, but the suspension has weakened with age. Helper springs, new spring shackles, and new shock absorbers will restore life to the suspension system.

Worn rollers and bunkers are almost standard on most used trailers. The rollers are standard items, and can be supplied by most trailer manufacturers. Your local lumberyard can supply wood with which to replace damaged or rotted wooden bunkers. Old carpet from a thrift shop can be cut up to provide covers for the bunkers.

Wheel bearings should be replaced as a matter of course unless you know the conditions of the trailer's previous use. Use new seals with the bearings, and follow the procedure illustrated in the maintenance section of this book.

Also inspect the coupler, and the winch and its line. Often these need only cleaning and lubrication in order to restore them to like-new condition, but if they do not appear to work properly, they should be replaced.

If the trailer has brakes, have a mechanic pull the wheel drums so lining can be checked, and replaced if necessary. Brake action also should be checked.

Try to have all your checks and inspections made before you pay for the trailer, then add the estimated cost of repairs to the trailer's purchase price. If many replacements and a lot of work are needed, it may be less expensive to buy a brand-new trailer.

2. Preparation

Once the trailer has been selected, it must be adjusted to provide an exact fit to your boat, to minimize any chance of hull distortion, and the adjustment must be such that the hitch weight works out to be about 5 to 7 per cent of the total load. Also, if the trailer has more than one axle, weight distribution must be such that each axle carries its rated share of the load.

Tongue weight is critical. Too much weight, or too little, will have an adverse effect on the trailer's ability to maintain a straight track behind the car, as well as on the behavior of the car itself. A trailer that yaws from side to side at highway speeds is dangerous. It literally can pull the car off the road, or into oncoming traffic. Tire pressure, which will be discussed later, is also a factor in helping the trailer maintain a straight track behind the towing vehicle.

A boat gets its best support from water. The object in setting up your trailer is to try to emulate this support as much as possible with the trailer's rollers and bunkers. This means it must be supported as evenly as possible along the line of the keel, along the chines near the stern, and at the transom where engine weight is concentrated.

Trailer Setup

If you buy the boat and trailer as a package from a dealer, the chances are that he will set up the trailer for you before he delivers the rig. If he has not done so, or if you have purchased boat and trailer separately, you will have to do your own setup.

Even if the dealer has done the job, it's a good idea to check everything out to make sure it is right. Occasionally a dealer in a hurry to prepare a lot of boats for his customers may not take the necessary trouble to provide an accurate job.

Start with a temporary setup that positions the boat so that rollers or bunkers at the rear of the trailer bed are directly under the transom. Be sure there's enough support under the keel and chines so the boat will not roll or shift. Now, with a normal load of gear aboard, in the position in which it normally will be carried, check the tongue weight.

Tongue weight can be checked with a common bathroom scale if 5 to 7 per cent of the total load will be less than 250 pounds. Place the scale on a box or other sturdy support that will put the trailer tongue at car-hitch height when the tongue rests on the scale platform. The scale reading is the tongue weight.

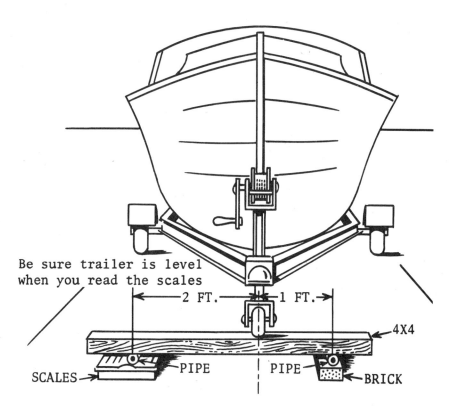

Figure 18. How to weigh trailer tongue with bathroom scale.

If yours is a large, heavy boat with a tongue weight that should be 250 pounds or more, set up a weighing rig as shown in Figure 18. Place a brick or a block of approximately the same thickness as the bathroom scales on the ground, spaced so the centerline of the block is exactly three feet from the center of the scale platform. Place a short length of pipe along each centerline, and rest a length of a 4″ x 4″ wood beam across the pipes.

Now support the trailer tongue over the 4″ x 4″ beam, with the trailer jack or another length of pipe, so the tongue is at the height of the car's hitch. It should be positioned one foot from the centerline of the block, 2 feet from the centerline of the scale.

To get the tongue weight, multiply the scale reading by three. For example, if the scale reads 120 pounds, the tongue weight is 360 pounds, which is just 7 per cent of a 5,000-lb. load.

If the tongue weight measured is greater than the 5 to 7 per cent figure you have computed based on total load weight, the load must be shifted to the rear of the trailer, or the trailer axle must be shifted forward, until the correct tongue weight is obtained. If measured tongue weight is too low, the load must be moved forward on the trailer, or the axle must be moved to the rear, to increase weight at the tongue (see Figure 19).

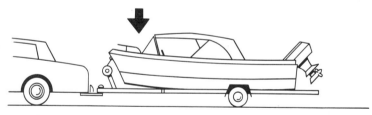

WEIGHT TOO FAR FORWARD. TOO MUCH TONGUE WEIGHT.

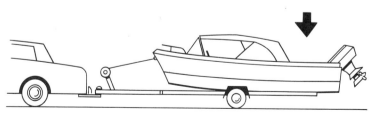

WEIGHT TOO FAR AFT. NOT ENOUGH TONGUE WEIGHT.

Figure 19.

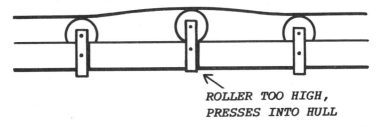

ROLLER TOO HIGH,
PRESSES INTO HULL

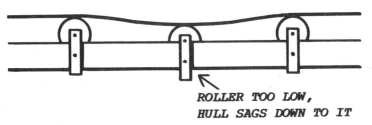

ROLLER TOO LOW,
HULL SAGS DOWN TO IT

Figure 20. Equal height of rollers is important.

When making trailer adjustments, it is recommended that socket wrenches, box wrenches, or open-end wrenches of the proper sizes be used for loosening and tightening of all adjustment bolts and nuts. An adjustable end wrench is acceptable, but never use pliers. You won't get bolts tight enough, and you'll gouge and disfigure them so that the correct wrenches won't grip properly. A Stillson (pipe) wrench will tighten nuts securely but it, too, will mutilate them.

Once proper tongue weight has been achieved, rollers and bunkers can be set up permanently. Rollers should be spaced evenly along the keel, and each roller should be snug against the keel. Each roller must carry its share of the weight. If a roller is slightly low, there's a tendency for the hull to sag in that area during periods of long storage. If a roller is too high, it can make a permanent indentation in the hull at that point (see Figure 20).

If your boat is an outboard, or an inboard with stern drive, be sure there is adequate support along the line of the transom where engine weight is concentrated. If the hull extends even a few inches beyond any supporting members, it may sag down and develop a permanent hook in the bottom which will cause the boat to porpoise badly when in operation (see Figure 21).

Figure 21. This outboard has proper support along the transom.

Side rollers or bunkers should be raised so that they are snug under the hull along the chine lines. On trailer models with adjusting arms, the bolts must be loose both at the pivot point and in the slotted holes before adjusting; retighten the bolts after the arms are properly positioned.

Where guide rollers are incorporated at the rear of the trailer to make boat loading easier, they should be adjusted under the transom so they also carry a portion of the load when the boat is on the trailer.

Next move the bow-stop winch support forward or backward as necessary, and adjust the stop up or down to provide a snug fit against the boat. Generally, the stop is a V-shaped member padded with rubber, and it should rest against the bow just below the boat's bow eye—the ring to which the winch line must be attached. Some trailers have a pair of rollers mounted on a swivel (see Figure 22). This can be adjusted so the bow eye is between the rollers.

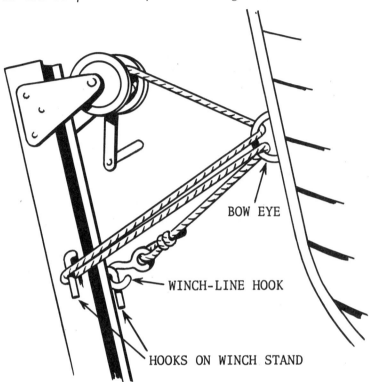

BOW EYE

WINCH-LINE HOOK

HOOKS ON WINCH STAND

Figure 22. Positioning the bow eye.

Boats built to Outboard Boating Club recommendations will have the bow eye 16 inches above the line of the keel if they are 16 feet or less in over-all length, and 20 inches above the line of the keel if they are more than 16 feet in length. Winch heights on most trailers are factory set for these bow-eye heights, so that the winch will be a few inches above the level of the bow eye. This makes for easiest launching and loading. If possible, adjust the winch height. If your bow eye is too high or too low, raise or lower the winch unit so the line will feed out about 3 inches above the center of the bow eye.

The boat is secured to the trailer when on the road by tie-downs at the stern, and one at the bow. Do not rely on the winch line to secure the bow of the boat to the trailer, although the arrangement shown in Figure 22 will hold the bow forward and down at the same time. Should the winch line fail, however, or the winch gear lock release, a sudden stop might result in having the boat ride up and over the bow stop. Use an extra length of line from the bow eye to the trailer tongue for the necessary security. A typical tie-down strap is shown in Figure 23. These should be used only when the rig is on the road. They should be set up so they are taut, but not putting a compression stress on the hull. In any case remove them if the boat is to be stored on the trailer for any length of time, for a prolonged stress could cause deformation of the hull.

Figure 23. A typical tie-down strap.

When the trailer is coupled to the car, be sure that the safety chain or chains are properly attached. If two chains are used, they should be crossed under the tongue to provide a cradle into which the tongue will drop should the coupling fail. If a single chain is long enough, it can be run from trailer to hitch and back again to provide the same sort of cradle (see Figure 24).

There's even a right way and a wrong way to do something as simple as attaching the S hook at the end of the chain to the car. If the hook is inserted through the hole from the top, a moderate

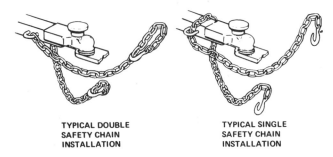

TYPICAL DOUBLE
SAFETY CHAIN
INSTALLATION

TYPICAL SINGLE
SAFETY CHAIN
INSTALLATION

Figure 24. Safety chain or chains should be properly attached.

bounce could cause it to jar loose. Insert the hook from the bottom of the hole, as illustrated in Figure 25, and nothing can shake it loose.

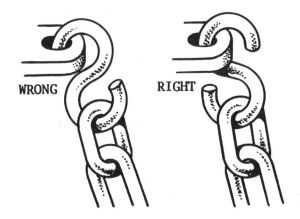

WRONG   RIGHT

Figure 25. Do it right!

Practice Maneuvers

If you never have driven with a trailer behind your car, your first trip should be to the local supermarket parking lot on a Sunday afternoon, or to any similar lot where there is plenty of room, marked lanes, and no interfering traffic.

Couple the trailer to your car, attach the safety chain, and plug in the electrical connector. Have someone check to make sure that clearance lights, taillight, stoplight, and turn signals all operate properly. Make sure all wheel lug bolts are tight. Check tire pressure in all tires to see that it is correct. Then, on your trip to the parking lot, remember that you will need to swing a little wider than you would with the car alone when turning corners, and that trailer weight behind the car requires a greater distance for stopping, even if the trailer is fitted with brakes.

Don't tailgate at any speed: This is good driving practice with or without a trailer, but doubly necessary when you have a trailer in tow. Should the vehicle in front of you make a sudden stop, you must have ample room to bring your car to a smooth, safe stop.

At the parking lot, use the lane lines as guides or set out boat cushions or similar objects as markers. Practice slow-speed turns, moving forward, to learn how far out you have to swing to avoid having the trailer cut the corner too sharply. A friend or family member acting as an outside observer is a help here, as also in the subsequent practice maneuvers.

Try pulling into parking spaces alongside a curb (you'll take up two spaces, of course. When you do this on a village or city street with metered parking, you'll have to pay for two spaces). Also practice pulling in between line markers and stop so that the trailer is at a predetermined point. Be prepared for parking requirements or restrictions you might find at any launching ramp.

The most important maneuver, however, is backing the trailer. Try backing in a straight line, very slowly, of course. It doesn't take much to have the trailer set off on its own course, and this can be very disconcerting as you try to bring it back into line. It's likely that at first any attempt to correct the path of the trailer will only send it even more in the wrong direction.

Backing a trailer is *easy*—once you get the hang of it. The secret is to turn the front wheels of the car in the "wrong" direction, as you back down. This pushes the trailer tongue *away* from the desired direction, with the result that the rear of the trailer turns *in* toward the desired direction.

As the trailer starts to line up with the desired course, straighten out the wheels on the car, then turn them in the right direction so the car actually follows the trailer around the turn (see Figure 26).

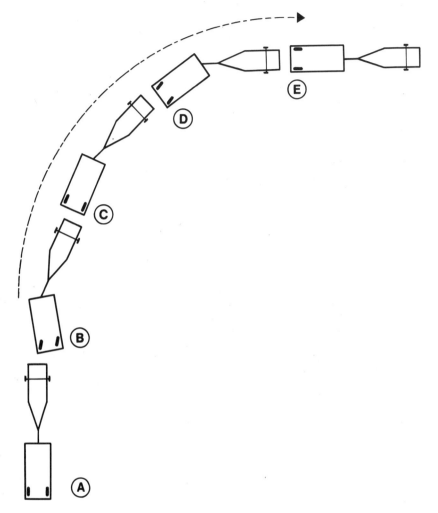

Figure 26. Relationship of car's front wheels to path taken by trailer when backing around a corner.

It's a help to place your hands on the *bottom* of the steering wheel, then move your hands in the same direction you want the trailer to turn as you start the maneuver (see Figure 27). This will take a fair amount of practice, during which you can determine what amount of steering action will produce how much turning action of the trailer.

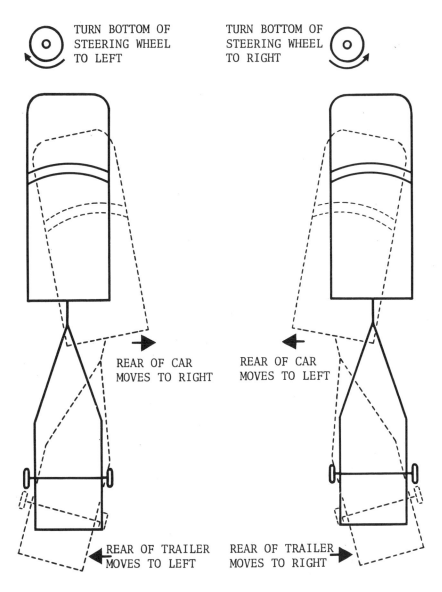

TURN BOTTOM OF
STEERING WHEEL
TO LEFT

TURN BOTTOM OF
STEERING WHEEL
TO RIGHT

REAR OF CAR
MOVES TO RIGHT

REAR OF CAR
MOVES TO LEFT

REAR OF TRAILER
MOVES TO LEFT

REAR OF TRAILER
MOVES TO RIGHT

Figure 27. When backing up, steer the car in the wrong direction to start the trailer in the right direction.

Avoid "jackknifing." This occurs when the trailer is at such a sharp angle behind the car that any further backing will push the trailer sideways, with possible damage to car, boat, and trailer. Your lookout should be able to warn you to stop if a jackknife is developing! Always maneuver slowly so that you can stop before any damage is done.

When you feel that you can control direction of the rig when in reverse, try backing it between lane markers, and into a curbside parking space. Before long you will find that you can place the trailer wherever you want it, and with a minimum of fuss. This practice will later save you time—and embarrassment—at the launching ramp when you prepare to launch your boat.

Preparation for the Road

So now your boat is properly secured to the trailer and you have practiced enough so that you are confident of your ability to handle the rig at the launching ramp. There are still a few things you will need to check, however, before you head for the waterfront—and these are checks you should make before every trip.

• Be certain that everything that is to be carried in the trailer is stowed securely. Lash down batteries, anchors, toolboxes, fuel tanks, and every other heavy item that could shift due to road shock, causing damage inside the boat. Distribute the load weight so that the tongue weight remains at the proper proportion to the total load on the trailer.

It may be that items normally carried on the boat while it's afloat will be carried in the car on the trip to the ramp; this would be the case if the trailer is loaded close to its capacity. On the other hand, it may be possible for you to stow camping gear and luggage in the boat itself if trailer capacity is adequate, leaving more room for the family to stretch out in the car.

• Check lists always are a good idea, even for a day's outing. You'll want to be sure you have all required safety equipment along, such as personal flotation devices (life jackets), flares, and so on. And those other items that obviously are necessary, even though not required by the Federal Government; namely, anchor and anchor line, mooring lines, compass, flashlight, and tools. For an extended trip add charts, food and water, sleeping bags, tent, galley equipment, fishing gear, and other items you will need.

• Remove navy top, canvas covers, bow pennant, and stern ensign if the boat is to be trailered at highway speeds. Going 50 or 55 m.p.h. into a 20 m.p.h. wind would subject these to far more of a beating than they are designed to take, and they would be sure to be damaged. In fact, it's a good practice to remove such items even before short hauls to the local ramp.

TABLE V

PRE-HIGHWAY CHECK LIST

I. Check for Initial Matching:
___ Are rollers, bolsters, and other contact points adjusted to boat contour?
___ When turned to maximum limit does any part of the boat or trailer contact towing vehicle?
___ Is there proper slack in safety chains to allow maximum turns?
___ Do lights, brakes, license, etc. meet state's legal requirements?
___ Is trailer balanced so that the hitch load is within the limits with fuel tanks either full or empty?

II. Check Before Every Trip:
___ Are all parts, nuts and bolts tight?
___ Are all moving parts lubricated and operating properly?
___ Are tires inflated to correct pressure?
___ Are all boat tie-downs properly secured?
___ Are all lights operating properly?
___ Is trailer hitch tight and safety chains secure?
___ Are brakes operating properly?
___ Is motor tight on transom and locked or secured in position with sufficient road clearance?
___ Are locks on winch, bunk, or tilt mechanisms in proper position?
___ If baggage or equipment is carried in the boat, is the load evenly distributed and secured?
___ Are wheel bearings properly lubricated? (Check periodically.)
___ Are gas tanks tightly closed? It is recommended that tanks be left empty on long trips and filled upon arrival at destination.

NOTE: It is recommended that Part II be checked periodically while on trip.

• Go over the boat, trailer, and hitch, using the Boating Industry Association's recommended check list as given here in Table V. Most important is the tire pressure, as improperly inflated tires will have an adverse effect on trailer behavior when on the road. Also, they're subject to more rapid wear and more prone to blowouts than are tires inflated to the correct pressure. Table VI shows recommended tire pressures.

• If your boat is an outboard, tilt the motor up and turn it to one side. To protect it from road debris, be sure it will not unlock from the tilt position and slam down against the transom. There are some commercially available lower-unit supports (see Figure 28) which are made for this purpose. *NOTE:* Never tow an outboard with the motor in the "down" position.

TABLE VI

TIRE LOAD CAPACITY AT VARIOUS INFLATIONS

Tire Size	Ply Rating	30	35	40	45	50	55	60	65	70	75	80	85
4.80/4.00 x 8	2	380											
4.80/4.00 x 8	4	380	420	450	485	515	545	575	600				
5.70/5.00 x 8	4		575	625	665	710							
6.90/6.00 x 9	6		785	850	915	970	1030	1080					
6.90/6.00 x 9	8		785	850	915	970	1030	1080	1125	1175	1225	1270	
20 x 8.00-10	4	825	900										
20 x 8.00-10	6	825	900	965	1030	1100							
20 x 8.00-10	8	825	900	965	1030	1100	1155	1210	1270	1325			
20 x 8.00-10	10	825	900	965	1030	1100	1155	1210	1270	1325	1370	1420	1475
4.80/4.00 x 12	4	545	550	595	635	680	715	755	790				
5.30/4.50 x 12	4	640	700	760	810	865	915						
5.30/4.50 x 12	6	640	700	760	810	865	915	960	1005	1045	1090	1135	
6.00 x 12	4	855	935	1010									
6.00 x 12	6	855	935	1010	1090	1160	1230	1290					
6.50 x 13	6	895	980	1060	1130	1200	1275						

NOTE: This table gives load capacities per tire for various tire sizes and inflation pressures (measured cold before starting). The underlined value on each line is the maximum inflation-load value for that tire at highway speeds.

Spare Parts

A spare wheel, with properly inflated tire, can be mounted on the trailer frame at any spot where it will clear the hull, and can be easily reached if needed. Better still, carry it in the car's trunk, to prevent theft.

If your trailer is not equipped with a tongue jack, invest in a good scissor or hydraulic jack that can be used to raise the tongue to a convenient height for hookup to the car, or for storage. It also should retract far enough to slip under the trailer axle when a tire is flat. Even if you have a tongue jack, you'll need an axle jack for use when fixing flats.

Figure 28. Lower-unit supports protect motor.

Carry at least one spare bulb of every type that is used on your trailer. A compartmented plastic box can hold these, with a slip of paper in the bottom of each compartment to identify the bulb and its use. Add spare bulbs for your car's lights, and spare fuses for both car and trailer.

A few spare connectors are a good investment, too. Pre-wire them with short lengths of color-coded wiring. When an old connector goes bad, clip it off and hook on a new one, using the crimp-on tool.

Other spares to carry are items for the boat itself, such as propeller, shear pins, cotter keys, starter rope, running-light bulbs, fuses, and so on.

3. On the Road

When hauling a trailer in local slow-speed traffic, keep in mind the principles you learned in your practice at the parking lot. You will need more distance to bring your rig to a stop. You will need more room at corners when making a turn. Figure 29 illustrates the paths taken by car and trailer when turning a corner the wrong way and the right way.

Adjust side mirrors so you can see what is behind the trailer, as well as what is on each side of it. Of course, you won't be able to see what is immediately behind the trailer—for two or three car lengths—but you should be able to tell when traffic is moving up behind you.

When you make a right-hand turn, make sure the lane to your left is clear, because you will have to swing into it slightly in order to start the turn. Be sure your turn signal indicates a right turn. A left turn at an intersection usually poses no problem in clearance.

Always maintain enough distance behind a vehicle to bring your rig to a smooth, safe stop in an emergency. A good rule of thumb is to double the distance you would leave if you were driving the car without the trailer. That distance, of course, should be one car length for every 10 m.p.h. of car speed. You never know when the driver ahead is going to have to make a panic stop. On wet pavements or in conditions of limited visibility, use added care.

Out on the open highway be content to stay within speed limits for vehicles towing trailers. Usually these are posted, but you should know what they are for your area even if they are not posted. See Appendix A: State Trailer Requirements for each state's requirements regarding trailers.

54

Trailer speed limits often are 10 to 15 m.p.h. below those for cars, so get in the right-hand lane and *stay* there on super-highways. This permits faster cars to pass on your left with a minimum of interference to the flow of traffic. Only when you have a slower vehicle in front of you should you pull out into the left lane to pass, and then return to the right lane as soon as you

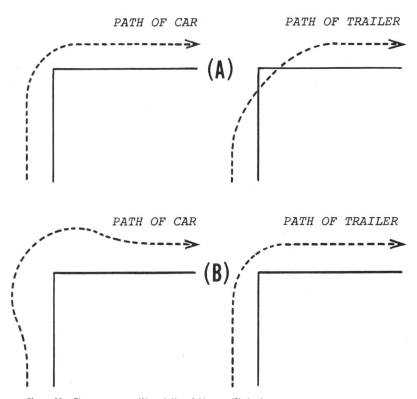

Figure 29. The wrong way (A) and the right way (B) to turn a corner.

are clear. Even if there are three or four lanes for traffic going in your direction, stay to the right. Vehicles trying to pass on your right create an unnecessary hazard.

By staying in the right-hand lane, you will be exercising courtesy as well as good driving practice.

On a two-lane highway (*i.e.*, one lane in each direction) when you see that traffic is piling up behind you, pull off the road at some convenient spot to allow the faster vehicles to pass. It may be necessary to do this every 20 minutes or so on a long stretch, but the drivers of the cars behind you will appreciate your courtesy.

At least once an hour, whether on superhighway or back road, pull off onto the shoulder of the road and check your rig. Again, follow the BIA check list as given in Table V, on page 51.

When you check tire pressure at such a roadside stop, it should be three to five pounds per square inch (psi) higher than it was when you checked at the start of your trip. This is caused by the heat build-up in the tire and is normal. Do not release air to reduce the pressure! If your stop is long enough for the tires to cool, you will see that the pressure will drop of itself. The tires are designed to give best performance and to wear better at the higher pressure.

Ample stopping distance becomes even more important at highway speeds, because if you hit something, you'll hit it harder. When necessary to slow down or stop, brake gently, with a pumping action. This not only gives you better control of car and trailer, but also prolongs the life of brake linings. Hard braking can cause your wheels to lose their contact with the road, and then you are in a skid with perhaps a ton or more of trailer and boat ready to slam into you from behind when the car slams into something in front of *it*.

This brings up another point. If your trailer is small, with no brakes at all, it might be possible to bring the car to a safe, fast stop only to have the trailer and boat surge forward over the hitch and into the car. Or, if the boat's bow is not properly secured, the boat could ride right up over the bow stop when you come to a sudden halt.

Under normal highway conditions, and at reasonable speeds you may find that the trailer tends to yaw or wander from side to side. Pull off the road to locate and correct the cause of the trouble. Check tire pressure. More often than not this is the culprit. One wheel is running softer than the other, creating a slight drag on that side of the trailer. Proceed at a moderate speed to the nearest gas station and bring up the pressure in the low tire to match the pressure in the other tire. On the other hand, you could reduce pressure in the high tire to match the low one, and then proceed to the gas station if there is one close at hand. Keep in mind that low pressure is the biggest cause of rapid tire wear and blowouts.

If tire pressure in the tires is found to be equal or nearly so, you can assume that tongue weight may be too little or too much at the hitch. Try moving some heavy items forward in the boat, and see if the trailer tracks any better. If it does, you're in luck. If it doesn't, try shifting weights aft in the boat to decrease tongue weight.

Should all your corrective measures fail, you can proceed at a moderate speed to minimize the errant behavior of the trailer. As soon as possible, however, have the rig checked by a boat or trailer dealer to determine the cause, and to provide a positive cure for the problem.

Keep in mind that a strong cross wind will tend to push the trailer to one side. The stronger the wind, the slower you may need to travel in order to keep the trailer under control. Don't confuse this action with the yawing that results from improper tire inflation or improper tongue weight.

On a long trip, include a rest stop for every two hours you are on the road. This is a standard practice for bus, truck, and other professional drivers. It gives you a chance to relax from the stress of driving. Of course, you can use these stops for trailer checks as well as meals, sightseeing, or whatever other activities may be in order.

Some Driving Tips

In mountainous or hilly country, keep your speed down when descending long inclines. Use a lower gear, if possible, to take advantage of the engine's braking action when your foot is off the gas pedal. Apply car and trailer brakes as gently and as sparingly as possible to avoid overheating them. Hot brakes tend to fade; you lose braking efficiency.

In any terrain, accelerate slowly and smoothly. It not only helps to save gas, but also reduces strain on the engine and transmission of your car. Avoid jack-rabbit starts, sudden acceleration, and hard stops that put a shock force on the hitch ball and trailer coupler.

If the temperature of the water in the radiator starts to rise when you're driving up a long, steep hill, pull off to the side of the road. With the brakes set and the transmission in neutral, "goose" the engine for a few seconds. With no load on the engine, the action of the fan pulling air through the radiator should reduce engine temperature. You can use this trick, too, when stuck in hot summer traffic—with or without the trailer.

However, if this doesn't work, shut the engine off and let it cool down naturally. This will also give you a chance to stretch, and to check your rig. If the car has boiled over, or is about to do so, do not remove the radiator cap until the engine has cooled down. Water in the cooling system is under pressure, and this pressure is increased when steam is present. You could be scalded by the steam and hot water spurting from under the cap when it is loosened.

Even when you feel the system has cooled to the point where it is safe to remove the cap, take a simple precaution. Cover the cap with a wadded-up old towel or other heavy cloth, then turn the cap slowly until it hits its first "detent," the point where resistance is felt. Any steam or water that is released at this point will be absorbed by the towel. Then turn the cap the remainder of the way, and lift it off.

Never permit anyone to ride in the boat when it is being towed on the trailer. This is a dangerous practice, and in most states it is illegal.

Always check your rear-view mirrors before pulling out of a parking space alongside a curb, before changing lanes when on the highway, before making any sort of turn, and before coming to a quick stop. When pulling a boat trailer you cannot maneuver as quickly as you can with the car alone, and you need to know traffic conditions to the rear as well as to each side.

Always give the coupler a final check before you drive off. Make sure that it is properly tightened or latched. If a locking pin is used, make sure that it is in place and secured.

Boat Trailer Camping

With a pair of bunks, a galley, and an enclosed head, a trailered boat of moderate size can serve as a roadside camper for a couple when on long road trips. Larger boats may even be able to accommodate a small family. By using your boat as a camper, you can bypass hotels and motels, as well as the expensive restaurants, along your route. And you can enjoy all the recreational benefits that accrue to the regular land-locked camper.

Boat size is fairly important. An 18-foot runabout with seats that fold into lounges is about the minimum. A cruiser of 20 feet or more in length is best. The 25-footer is about the maximum, in terms of trailerability and ease of handling at the launching ramp. It, of course, offers the most comfort to the campers.

Sleeping comfort is a first consideration. Even berths that seem quite comfortable when the boat is rocking quietly at a mooring may turn out to be hard and uncompromising when the boat is rigid on its trailer. To remedy this, thick polyurethane pads in 4-inch slabs can be cut to fit your bunk contours, and placed right under the existing cushions.

Also, you may find that bunks that are level when the boat is afloat are high at either the head or foot when the boat is on the trailer. For this, uncouple the trailer from the car, and use your tongue jack to adjust height at the tongue so that the bunks are level.

A cruiser, of course, provides shelter in its cabin, but for a runabout you may need to rig a navy top of ample length to keep out rain. Supplement this top with enclosure curtains for added weather protection.

The chances are good that your boat's windshield and side windows are higher from the ground than a standard camper's windows, but you may still need to add curtains for privacy. You'll find the curtains helpful when afloat, too—at crowded marinas, and marinas where pier lights are kept on brightly all night as a security measure.

The galley may well need no alteration for on-the-road use. If you have an ice chest, keep it loaded with ice cubes to avoid food spoilage. If yours is a dockside-powered electric refrigerator, stock it with ice cubes to keep the contents cool until you reach a campsite that provides electrical service. Even a 12-volt refrigerator operated off the boat's battery can be helped along with the ice-cube treatment. If your boat is new, and you're just fitting out the galley, use of a top-loading ice chest or refrigerator is recommended. This type does not lose its cool when opened as quickly as will a side-opening model, and there's no chance of its door accidentally flying open when you bounce across the wake of another boat.

To your galley gear you can add a portable backyard barbecue grill—one that folds and stows aboard the boat when not in use. Many campsites provide grills or fireplaces, but many do not. Thus, the barbecue grill is a pleasant supplement to the boat's stove.

Federal and state requirements for marine toilets have been in a muddle for years, and may remain so for some time to come. Under present regulations, you can't use a toilet that needs an outside source of water, or one that discharges overboard—even through a macerator-chlorinator unit. Get a recirculating toilet with its own water supply, such as the Monomatic, or a portable unit such as the Porta-Potti or Sani-Potti. Fortunately, many state parks, trailer parks, private campsites, and even filling stations have "sanitary dumping facilities," where all of these units can be emptied. Indeed, the small Sani-Potti types can be emptied into a standard toilet with no fuss. The incinerator type of toilets that are available for campers are not recommended for marine use at this time.

It's not the easiest thing in the world to climb into the cockpit of a boat when the boat is on a trailer. You will need a boarding ladder of some sort. The ladder shown here in Figure 30 works well. One boatman, a pioneer in the art of boat trailer-camping, cut the rear legs off a six-foot aluminum stepladder, then added a length of split plastic hose to the rear edge of the top step to keep it from marring the hull.

Your boarding ladder can be lashed to the trailer frame or under cockpit gunwales when not in use. When you're aboard the boat at night in a campsite or rest area, pull the ladder up for security. No one could climb aboard from the trailer fender without creating considerable disturbance.

If your have the electric Monomatic-type toilet, plus a refrigerator that operates off the boat's battery and also cabin lights that you use at night, a good investment will be a small generator hooked to a suitable battery charger.

Bugs ashore can be just as annoying as bugs afloat, so screens, netting, bug sprays, and insect repellent will be advisable even if you do not use the boat as a camper. You can buy mosquito nets

Figure 30. Boarding ladder in position. It can be raised at night for security.

that can be suspended over the bunks, as a minimum, or add window screens and enclosure screens that seal bugs out of the entire boat. Rig them, give the interior a shot of bug spray to eliminate all those that are inside, and you should have an insect-free night.

Regular cockpit enclosure curtains also will keep bugs out, but they may leave the interior unbearably stuffy on a hot night. Conversely, on a cool night, they will keep the interior comfortable long after outside temperature has become quite chilly.

CAMPSITES

On a long road trip, a camper's guidebook such as "Woodall's" is a real help. The shoreside equivalent of a cruising guide, this book lists locations of campsites and roadside rest areas, fees, if any, and the facilities available at each site. Thus, you can plan your trip so that you will arrive at sites that feature such things as laundry, shower, and sanitary dumping facilities, as you need them.

A word of caution about campsite—and marina—laundromats. Often these are subject to heavy use, and the water is not as hot as that used in standard commercial coin-operated laundries. Germs and bacteria can transfer from one load of clothes to the next, so be sure to add a suitable disinfectant to your wash water.

Roadside rests do not offer many of the facilities found at most campsites. Some are just a parking area alongside the road, others have picnic tables and benches; some have telephones and toilets. In most you can stop overnight. Some states prohibit this, and signs at the area will let you know if you may stay or not. A big advantage to the roadside rest is that there is no charge. They are marked on the state road maps available from gas stations, and usually they are spaced close enough together along the major highways so that you can find one no matter how long or how short you want to make your day's run.

Campsite etiquette is similar to that observed in the marina. Keep kids and pets under control. In the evening, keep lights, voices, and radios low so the early-bedtime infants can get to sleep. Deposit garbage and trash in the containers provided for the purpose, and don't leave any sort of mess behind you when you depart. If you have a campfire, grill or fireplace fire, be sure that it is completely out before you leave. Last but not least: Respect the privacy of your neighbors.

You will make friends along your way ashore, just as on your cruises afloat. The use of a boat as a camper is rare enough so that you will have an icebreaker. It's fairly large as a conversation piece, and most certainly will attract the curious. If you enjoy meeting and talking to people, you will find the trip to your launching site every bit as much fun as the boating itself.

4. At the Launching Ramp

When you arrive at the ramp, do not be in too much of a hurry to get your boat into the water. First, pull off to one side—many ramps have prelaunch parking areas—or into the parking area and get your boat ready.

Even if the launching ramp is clear, and you are familiar with it, don't back down to the water's edge before you start your boat preparation. You could block the way for others who are ready to launch.

There are two reasons for taking your time and not dunking your boat right away. First, in your hurry you may overlook something essential, such as closing the transom drain on the boat or unhooking the trailer wiring from the car. Secondly, you need to give trailer wheel bearings a chance to cool down. Immerse a hot bearing assembly in cold water, and the air in the bearing housing will contract rapidly, creating a low-pressure system that literally sucks in water through even the most watertight seals. Water rapidly destroys the effectiveness of bearing lubricants, so that the bearings burn out when you hit the road again.

Preparation for Launching

If the ramp is an unfamiliar one, it's a good idea to stay to one side (even after you are ready to launch) and watch the launching of one or two other boats in order to get a good idea of what the local problems are. How far is it necessary to back the trailer into the water? Does one section of the ramp look as if it will be better than another? Is there any problem with wind or current?

63

Is there a pier at which you can lie while loading gear onto your boat?

Remove any gear from the boat that is to be stored in the car. Rig tops, ensign, and pennants as necessary or desirable. Bring picnic hampers, fishing tackle, life preservers, and similar gear to the loading pier if one is present. It's easier to hand down such items to someone in the boat than to hoist them up to it while it is still on the trailer.

Make up a check list you can follow that covers the gear, trailer, and boat preparation, and your normal launching procedures.

Essentially, you back the boat trailer down to within a few feet of the water, and set your parking brake. Your crew can help to guide you as you back down so you wind up with your rig perpendicular to the water's edge. Or, if you have a pickup truck or one of the big station wagons with a bumper hitch in front, you hitch the trailer to the front of the vehicle and back it down while you drive forward.

Now, disconnect the wiring plug between car and trailer (see Figure 31). Remove the trailer taillight and brake-light assem-

Courtesy Chrysler Marine

Figure 31. Disconnecting the wiring plug is a simple operation.

blies if this is possible, and cover the connector plugs with plastic electrician's tape to help keep water out of the contacts. Salt water, brackish water, and even heavily polluted fresh water are all extremely corrosive to electrical systems.

Remove the transom tie-down straps or chains (see Figure 32), and the safety line between the bow eye and trailer tongue. Be sure the transom drain plug is closed securely.

Courtesy Chrysler Marine

Figure 32. Remove transom tie-down straps or chains.

Rig a line to the boat's bow cleat, and a second line to a stern cleat on the appropriate-side if two lines are needed to control the boat in a cross wind or current. Use the bow line, in any case, to make sure the boat doesn't drift away once it is in the water.

Launching the Boat

Now release the car's parking brake and back the trailer down until the rear rollers are barely under water (see Figure 33). Have someone hold the guide line, while you disconnect the winch line from the bow eye, and put the boat into the water.

Figure 33. Ready to launch.

If the ramp angle is very slight, you may find it necessary to back the rig down until almost the entire trailer is immersed. For those with the drive-on type of trailer, this will be the standard procedure. Such owners then start the boat's engine, unhook the bow line, and back off the trailer.

Many boatmen with standard trailers make it a practice to back far enough down the launching ramp to drive the boat off the trailer. If you go this route, stop the trailer when the motor's lower unit is immersed far enough that cooling water will be picked up. Start the motor, and allow it to warm up. Then you can back the trailer down the rest of the way—have a crew member unhook the winch line—and drive the boat off the trailer.

If, for any reason, the motor doesn't start, you can pull the rig up the ramp and off to one side where you can check it out. This way, you won't have cast loose from the trailer, and then found out your motor was inoperative.

Even if you launch your boat by pushing it off the trailer, you can still start the motor before the boat is in the water, just to make sure it is in running condition. Be sure to shut it off, however, as soon as it starts!

In some cases it may be necessary to uncouple the trailer from the car and raise the tongue in order for the boat to slide into the water. It will help if you can place a flat rock or similar object under the trailer jack, and use this to lift the tongue.

Once the boat is afloat, lead it over to the loading area and secure it. Your crew can then load any additional gear aboard it while you drive car and trailer clear of the ramp (see Figure 34). If the trailer has been immersed in salt water, it's a good idea to give it a quick hosing with fresh water; most modern ramps have fresh-water taps available for this purpose, but the chances are you'll have to supply your own hose.

Park the rig in a lot designated for this purpose, or in a convenient spot that doesn't interfere with ramp activity if there is no designated parking lot. If your coupler can be locked, lock the trailer to the car, and lock up the car itself.

Courtesy Chrysler Marine

Figure 34. A crew member secures boat while trailer is driven away.

There are places where you can get the boat from the trailer into the water without use of a launching ramp. That is when a lift is used. Straps are passed under the hull of your boat and are attached to the hoist line(s). The boat is then lifted off the trailer, moved out over the water, and lowered gently into the water. Fees for this service may be either on a flat-rate basis, or so much per foot of boat length.

Retrieving the Boat

Hauling the boat back onto the trailer is more than just the reverse of launching it. For one thing, it's usually more difficult— at least to the extent of pulling it uphill onto the trailer with your winch.

If you are in a busy boating area, you may want to time your arrival either before or after the peak haul-out period when the ramp action is fairly frantic. You need time to do the job properly, rinse off your rig, and secure your gear without being rushed by the outfit behind you.

Start by pulling up at the ramp's loading pier, if one is available. Your crew can unload all the gear while you bring the trailer into position on the ramp.

Check to make sure the trailer is securely coupled to the car, and that the safety chains are in place. The wiring harness should be disconnected from the car's electrical system, and trailer lights removed, if they are of that type. Cover exposed wiring connectors with plastic electrician's tape to seal out water.

Back the trailer down to the water, just as for launching, until the rear rollers are barely submerged. Use a line attached to the boat's bow to bring it alongside the trailer, then attach the trailer winch line to the boat's bow eye. It may be necessary to rig a line to the stern of the boat to help keep it under control in a cross current or cross wind.

If it is your practice to drive the boat onto the trailer, or if you have a trailer specifically built for this, you will have to back the trailer far enough into the water to allow the boat to move onto the trailer under its own power (see Figure 35).

Regardless of whether you drive your boat onto the trailer or haul it up with the winch, you still have to line it up with the center line of the trailer so that it will load properly. When the

Figure 35. Successive stages in driving boat onto submerged trailer.

boat's weight is fully on the trailer, the rollers and bunkers should contact the hull exactly where they were before the boat was launched. Again, use both bow and stern lines, if necessary, to maneuver the boat into position behind the trailer, and to hold it in alignment as the winch is cranked.

Remember that the winch line is under a great deal of tension, and that if it should break, its whiplike action could injure you or your crew. Keep everyone clear of the line!

Fender guides can be a real help in centering a boat on a submerged trailer bed. The guide shown was rigged from an old car radio antenna; details of its simple construction are shown in Figure 36. The complete guide is shown in Figure 37. Most drive-on trailers have some form of such guides. There was one boatman who managed to bolt lengths of steel pipe upright on his fenders to act as guides, but the combination of their weight and the vibration on the road literally tore them out of the fenders, along with sizable chunks of the fenders themselves.

Haul or drive the boat up until it is snug against the bow stop, and secure it temporarily by locking the winch. It is recommended that you have a short length of line running from the tongue to the bow eye to help take the strain, as this is the only point at which the boat is connected with the trailer until it is up the ramp.

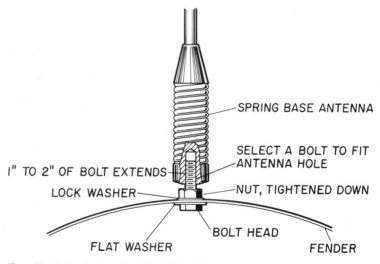

SPRING BASE ANTENNA

SELECT A BOLT TO FIT
ANTENNA HOLE

I" TO 2" OF BOLT EXTENDS

NUT, TIGHTENED DOWN

LOCK WASHER

BOLT HEAD

FLAT WASHER

FENDER

Figure 36. Schematic shows simple installation of fender guide.

Figure 37. Spring-base replacement antenna bolts to trailer fender as guide. This idea was developed by Glenn Hensley as an aid to owners of trailerable sailboats with retractable keels.

Figure 38. Crew members aid in centering boat on submerged trailer.

Now put the car's transmission into its lowest range, and pull the rig slowly up the ramp until it is clear of the water. Stop, set the parking brake, and check the position of the boat on the trailer. If it's just a little out of alignment, you may be able to jockey it into position. If you can't, or if it's badly out of alignment, back down the ramp, launch the boat, and reload it again.

If you are satisfied with the loading, open the transom drain, proceed up the ramp, and off to one side where you can complete your preparations for the road. Give the boat and trailer a good hosing with fresh water; being sure to clean salt from all metal surfaces, including chrome and aluminum.

Secure the outboard motor's lower unit in its trailering position, and attach transom tie-down straps or chains. Install the bow safety line from bow eye to trailer tongue if you have not done so already. Clean and dry the electrical connectors, and hook up all trailer lights.

If you have any reason to suspect that water has entered the trailer wheel bearings, this is the time to remove them and repack them with fresh grease. Watertight bearing seals of the "Bearing Buddy" type go a long way in eliminating this problem, but if there's any cause for doubt, repack the bearings.

Courtesy **Motor Boating & Sailing**

Figure 39. Mainsheet and boom are used to control mast descent after haul out of this sailboat. Mast is then disconnected at step and brought aft so that upper section of mast rests in support at bow of the boat. On the boat in background, the heel of the mast has been brought forward to bow bracket.

Follow your regular pre-departure list for loading and safety checks, and then you are ready for the trip home or to the next launching area. *NOTE:* Unstep the mast of a trailerable sailboat when the boat is on the trailer. Don't try it while the boat is still in the water where boat movement could cause you to lose the whole rig overboard. *When retrieving or launching such a boat, make sure there are no overhead power lines that the mast could strike.*

Unusual Ramp Conditions

Not all ramps are wide and paved, gentle inclines where there's ample maneuvering space for rig, good traction for your car's powered wheels, and just the right amount of slope to make launching and retrieval a textbook operation.

Instead, your ramp may be an old, unpaved road that leads down into a lake created by a dam and impoundment system, or it may even be a stretch of beach. You may have ramp that's fine at high tide but ends a few feet short of the water at low tide. Mud, sand, and/or rocks can interfere with your car's traction and cause delays.

Before you launch, plan exactly what you are going to do, both at the launching itself, and at the later retrieval. Ask yourself questions like these: Is there room to maneuver so you can back down? Will you have to uncouple the trailer, reverse it, and then reverse the car itself and re-hookup before you can back down? Are there large rocks that should be moved from the path of the rig? Are there soft spots in the sand where the trailer or car could bog down, and can you be guided around them?

Sometimes, when you have run out of good traction under the car's rear wheels, it will be necessary to uncouple the trailer from the car when still short of the water, and push it down by hand. A trailer tongue jack with wheel is handy here, but you and your crew will probably have to support some of the tongue weight yourselves in order to keep the little wheel from bogging down in soft ground, mud or sand. If the incline is so steep that you would not be able to control the trailer as it backs down, use blocks or rocks to secure the car's wheels, and secure the boat's bow eye to the trailer tongue or winch stand with a short length of line. Disconnect the winch line from the boat and attach it to the car's bumper or other suitable spot. Uncouple the trailer, and let out line from the winch to ease trailer and boat down into the water.

In places where there's tidal action, you may find launching and retrieving are easiest at high tide, so you will time your activities at the ramp to coincide with high tide. In some cases, however, a difference in the incline of the ramp may give you a better angle at low tide.

Fortunately, most ramps today do not present special problems such as this. If you like to get off the beaten track, however, you should make a careful survey of your ramp site before you launch your boat. Your objective is to get it into the water without fuss or damage, and you'll want to get it back out again later.

5. Storing Your Boat

One of the big advantages with a trailer rig is that you don't have to worry about a marina slip or mooring. Instead, you can bring the boat right home with you. Your driveway or yard is your home port. Instead of mooring at the end of the day, you park.

Temporary Storage

Pick a parking spot for the trailer that is as level and flat as possible, and out of the way of normal driveway and yard traffic. It should not be necessary to move the trailer each time you want to put your car in the garage.

Avoid picking a spot that's under a fruit tree—or under any tree—if possible. Keeping the boat clear of leaves and twigs is bad enough, but fallen fruit often will leave hard-to-remove stains on the boat. Any debris of this type that gets into the boat can clog limber holes and the transom drain.

You should be able to back your trailer into its parking spot with a minimum of maneuvering, and without damage to shrubs or trees on your property.

When you uncouple the car from the trailer, provide some support for the trailer tongue. Don't let it drop into the dirt where it may be damaged or pick up dirt that might prevent proper attachment to the hitch ball. Use your trailer jack, concrete blocks, or similar objects to brace the tongue at an angle that will allow water in the boat to run to the rear and out the transom drain.

While water may not harm the bilge of a fiberglass boat, it can stagnate and turn foul in a very short time, and the odor is hard to remove. In a wood boat, trapped moisture is conducive to rot.

You are really fortunate if you have a carport or garage in which you can keep both the car and trailer.

Courtesy Mercury Marine
Figure 40. Trailer blocked for long-term storage to keep weight off the wheels and tires. Small board under tongue jack wheel distributes weight so the wheel will not dig down into asphalt. It is important that such a block be used if the trailer is parked on a lawn.

Be sure your chosen parking space allows the trailer to sit level, from side to side. If the trailer is left in the yard, you can set bricks or small patio blocks into the ground in the spots where the wheels will rest. You don't want the trailer leaning to one side, and thus putting a distorting strain on both the boat and the trailer's suspension.

Whenever your trailer is parked, with the boat on it, slacken or remove the tie-downs and the bow safety line. These, too, put a strain on the hull that could cause distortion if they are left in place over a long period of time.

Long-Term Storage

At the end of your boating season, or at any time when you won't be doing any boating for a few months, take these extra steps to protect both boat and trailer.

● Remove the outboard motor, if you have this type of power, along with portable fuel tanks, batteries, and other heavy objects.

• Place concrete blocks or axle jacks under the trailer axles to take the strain off tires and running gear—again making sure the rig is level from side to side, and that the tongue is raised high enough so that rain water or melted snow will drain out the transom (see Figure 40).

• With the trailer blocked for storage, remove as much of its electrical gear as possible for storage indoors. The same applies to the boat electric parts, too. A warm, dry atmosphere reduces the chance of corrosion. Dampness accelerates electrical system corrosion.

• Also remove from the boat anything else that is best stored indoors, including the compass, anchor, and mooring lines. Take off any deck hardware that needs repair, replating, or replacement.

• Make up a list of off-season repairs that need to be done on the boat, new gear to be purchased, or alterations to be made. You'll be ready to head for the launching ramp on the first nice day of the next season.

Many boatmen rig a cover over boat and trailer to keep out debris, rain, and snow. The trouble with this, unfortunately, is that many such covers also keep out air. In these cases there's no ventilation to dry out trapped moisture or even moisture that condenses out of the air. Remember that it is such moisture that accelerates metal corrosion and promotes wood rot.

Set up your cover so that air vents are provided, either by lengths of stove pipe extending through suitable holes, or by flaps or spaces that allow air to circulate while keeping rain and snow out. Support the cover so that it will not sag and form big pockets where rain water or snow will collect.

During winter months, check the leveling of the boat occasionally. The alternate freezing and thawing that takes place in cold weather can allow ground to settle under one or more of the supports, thus throwing the trailer off balance. In such cases use wedges, or make jack adjustments, to effect corrections.

Be sure to follow the trailer maintenance procedures outlined in the next chapter. Winters can be hard on a trailer that's sitting out in the open. The preventive steps you take in the fall provide assurance that you will be ready to roll in the spring.

6. Maintenance

With a few preventive maintenance procedures followed as a matter of routine, a good trailer can last indefinitely. The deteriorating forces that need to be forestalled are corrosion, maladjustment of components, and normal wear resulting from use.

Tools

Start by carrying and using the right tools. They make work much easier, and they are less apt to damage fittings or your fingers. As noted earlier, end wrenches or box wrenches of the proper sizes are best for all roller, bunker, and other adjustments to the trailer frame. Adjustable end wrenches are a second best, and should be of good quality if used. Cheap ones won't hold adjustment; they'll slip, cause the rounding of corners of nuts, and give you skinned knuckles to boot.

Never use pliers of any sort on nuts and bolts. If you're tightening a fastening, you won't get it tight enough; if you're trying to loosen a tight fastening, you'll gouge and disfigure it to the point where no wrench will fit it, and the chances are that you'll not be able to budge it, anyhow.

You should carry a screwdriver or screwdrivers that will enable you to remove lenses from trailer lights so you can get to the bulbs and wiring. Also, as mentioned earlier, it's a good idea to invest in one of those wire stripper/crimper tools and a supply of crimp-on connectors. With these you can make proper, professional repairs to damaged or defective wiring.

A tool that is a must is a lug wrench that fits the lug nuts on your trailer wheels. Why not get one of those four-ended ones, so that it will fit both the trailer and your car? It always will be with you, in the car's trunk (see Figure 41).

Be sure you have all the tools that are needed for removing and replacing the wheel bearings; a screwdriver for prying off hubcaps and bearing cover, pliers for the cotter key, and a wrench of proper size for the axle nut. Carry some rags, too, for use in cleaning bearings, bearing housing, and axle before repacking with fresh grease. Don't save the used rags, they're a fire hazard; dispose of them in a metal container.

Courtesy Chrysler Marine

Figure 41. Typical tool assortment for a trailer.

A roll of electrician's plastic tape should be in your tool chest, along with a tube of liquid rubber. The liquid rubber is used to make a seal around wiring where it enters the housing of a light unit in order to keep water out if the light must be submerged.

Maintenance Procedures

Your fight against corrosion starts with the fresh-water rinse you give your rig every time it's hauled out of salt or polluted water. Be sure the salt is cleaned off all exposed metal, including chrome.

If yours is an aluminum trailer, salt-water corrosion is not so much of a problem, as the alloys used are designed for use in a marine environment. Beware of alkalis, however, as these will attack this metal. It's unlikely that a boat trailer will see much action in a winter climate, but the calcium chloride used on roads to melt ice is an alkali, and if any gets splattered onto the trailer, it should be washed off.

Check your trailer carefully for areas where paint has chipped or worn away, permitting the bared iron or steel to rust. If possible, sand away all traces of rust or use one of the rust removers such as Naval Jelly. Repaint with a metal primer, and a compatible finish coat in a color to match the original finish. If it's not possible to remove all the rust, use a rust-inhibiting paint such as Rustoleum. Start with the heavy-duty primer, which is a dark, reddish brown. If the finish coat is to be a light color, use the aluminum finish as an intermediate coat to prevent the dark primer color from bleeding through.

A light coat of oil on chains, coupler, all exposed bolts and nuts, and similar non-finished metal will prevent rust. Use paste wax on chrome, and on the painted surfaces, too, as a protective coat. The surface that can't be attacked can't deteriorate.

Tire pressure should be checked frequently, before and during trips as noted earlier. The chart given in Table VI on page 52 should be used as your guide. Remember that the pressures given are "cold" readings. Pressure will increase, of course, with heat build-up in the tire during use.

Inspect tires for signs of uneven or excess wear. Have the wheels balanced, if necessary, and replace badly worn tires with new ones of proper size and type. Be sure new tires are designed for use on a trailer. There are utility tires of the same size, but they don't have the strength needed for highway use.

Check wheel lugs for tightness prior to each trip, and inspect the bolt circles—the wheel area around each bolt hole—for cracks or deformation. If either is present, replace the wheel; don't run on it. It could break off the hub while you're out on the highway, and you can imagine the mess that would result.

Carefully examine all running gear two or three times a season, and again before winter storage. Look for misalignment, weak springs, loose, worn, or leaking shock absorbers. Replace worn shackle bushings. Inspect and adjust the brake system in accordance with the manufacturer's instructions.

Lubricate rollers, but be sure to wipe off any oil that spills onto the rubber itself. Replace worn or damaged rollers, and use old carpeting to re-cover bunkers that have worn padding. For these operations, and for any painting to be done on the trailer frame, it may be necessary to "launch" the boat into your yard, or leave it at a mooring for a suitable length of time.

If you do "launch" your boat in your yard, the procedure will depend on space available, and the weight of the boat. A small, light boat can be simply pulled off the trailer and lowered to the ground. For a large boat, back the trailer into the space the boat will occupy, and push the boat back until the stern overhangs enough so that supports can be placed under it. Ease the trailer forward, while placing supports under the boat as necessary. Plan the whole operation in advance; have your supports made up and ready for placement; be sure they will be strong enough to hold the boat's weight, and that they won't slip or fall from under the hull.

WHEEL BEARINGS

Repacking wheel bearings is a fairly simple operation. It should be done whenever there's any chance that water may have entered the bearing housing, with twice a season as a minimum. It is most important to repack the bearings before any period of prolonged storage so that no residual moisture can rust the bearings solidly to the housing and axle.

Jack up the wheel and remove the hubcap and bearing-housing cover. (If you have the "Bearing Buddy" type of cover, follow the specific instructions furnished with the unit.) Remove the cotter key that passes through the bearing retainer nut and axle, then remove the nut with a wrench of proper size. If you wiggle the wheel slightly, the outer seal and bearings will slide out of the housing and can be removed. Slip off the wheel, and remove the inner bearings and seal.

The bearing units can be cleaned by dunking them in gasoline or other suitable solvent. Work outdoors, of course, and don't smoke. Clean old grease off the axle, and out of the bearing housing.

Repack the bearings with a lubricant such as Lubriplate Marine A or No. 70. Replace the grease seals if they appear to be worn. Now reassemble the wheel to the axle; be sure to install the

Figure 42. Repacking wheel bearings.

1. Pry off the grease retainer. If the wheel has a hubcap, remove it first.

Sequence of photos courtesy Mercury Marine

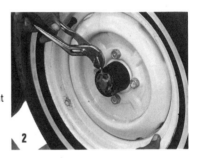

2. Bend the legs of the cotter key straight and remove it.

3. Long-nose pliers can be used to turn the wheel nut. However, a wrench is preferable.

Figure 42 (cont.)

4. Wiggle the wheel after the nut has been removed. This will work the bearing out from inside the housing.

5. Bearing assembly can now be pulled off the axle.

6. Slide wheel off the axle. Blocks used to support the axle can be seen. Do not leave axle supported only by a jack.

7. Using a drift pin, gently tap the inner bearing assembly to loosen it in its housing.

Figure 42 (cont.)

8. Pull the inner bearing and its seal out of the housing.

9. Use solvent to wash old grease from components. On the cloth are hubcap, axle nut, washer, inner seal, and cotter key.

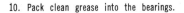

10. Pack clean grease into the bearings.

11. Replace inner bearing assembly (and the seal) on the inner side of the wheel.

Figure 42 (cont.)

12. Gently tap the seal back into place, flush with the edge of the housing. Use of new seals is recommended.

13. Replace outer bearing, seal, and axle nut. Tighten nut until it is snug. Wiggle wheel slightly to make sure all slack is out.

14. Back nut off until hole through axle lines up with notches in nut. Insert new cotter pin through the hole.

15. Bend out legs of cotter pin and replace grease retainer. Tap it gently into place to avoid damaging it.

seals with their lips facing in the right direction. Tighten the axle nut until it is snug and there is no play in the wheel when you try to wiggle it, then back it off just enough to permit a new cotter key to be inserted. Bend back the legs of the cotter key, and replace the bearing housing cap. Give the wheel a spin to make sure it turns freely, but without play. Also, check to see if the wheel is bent.

Lower and remove the jack; then repeat the procedure for the other wheel—or wheels, if you have a multiple-axle trailer.

Other Checks You Can Make

At storage time and at least once or twice during the season, lay a straightedge along the top of the axle, with the trailer loaded, to detect axle sag. Check cross frames on the trailer for sag in the midsection, which could lead to hull indentation at the chines. Most important is to sight lengthwise along the main frame to make sure it doesn't sag in the area behind the axle. A sag here indicates weakness caused by overload, or lack of strength in the frame member itself.

The presence of any of these conditions will mean the trailer should be replaced, as they do not lend themselves to correction. Go to a trailer of a higher capacity.

A vital link on all trailers is the coupler; another is the tilt hinge bolt on tilt-bed trailers. Check for wear, tightness, and fastenings to the tongue.

Be sure the hitch itself is tight on the car. The ball should stand vertical when the trailer weight is on it.

Inspect the winch rope for wear, and for the attachment of the winch hook. Replace the line if it is worn. Also check the bow eye on the boat itself, to make sure that it is securely fastened.

The best way to make certain that all your maintenance jobs are done, and done at the right time, is to make up a check list that suits your rig, *and follow it.*

Appendixes

A. State Trailer Requirements

The following table presents a digest of each state's requirements for trailer registration, and the speed limits on state highways. Most states have requirements, in addition to those shown. covering speed limits on different types of roads, trailer light location, trailer width, height, and length; hitches, safety chains, and trailer brakes.

A national 55-m.p.h. speed limit was established as a fuel conservation measure in 1974. This supersedes the maximum speed limits shown in the table that are above the 55-m.p.h. limit. However, it is expected the speed limits shown will go back into effect when, and if, the national 55-m.p.h. limit is rescinded.

Your best source of current information on all these requirements is the *Handbook of Boating Laws* for your area, published by the Outboard Boating Club of America, 333 N. Michigan Ave., Chicago, IL 60601. The *Handbook* is available in four regional editions:

Northeastern States: Connecticut, Delaware, District of Columbia, Maine, Maryland, Massachusetts, New Hampshire, New Jersey, New York, Pennsylvania, Rhode Island, Vermont, West Virginia ($1.95).

Southern States: Alabama, Arkansas, Florida, Georgia, Louisiana, Mississippi, North Carolina, Oklahoma, South Carolina, Tennessee, Texas, Virginia ($1.95).

North Central States: Illinois, Indiana, Iowa, Kansas, Kentucky, Michigan, Minnesota, Missouri, Nebraska, North Dakota, Ohio, South Dakota, Wisconsin ($1.00).

Western States: Alaska, Arizona, California, Colorado, Hawaii, Idaho, Montana, Nevada, New Mexico, Oregon, Utah, Washington, Wyoming ($1.00).

It is recommended that you obtain and study the edition for your area, as it covers all the legal requirements of the respective states for pleasure boating.

In the table, note that most states base the license fee on trailer weight, which may be empty weight, gross weight, or net weight. In this case both gross weight and net weight refer to total of trailer and maximum load. Many states did not indicate to the Outboard Boating Club which weight should be used. In any case it is advisable to check with the issuing office so that you will be sure to provide the right figures on your application.

Where the table refers to a county clerk or county treasurer as the issuing officer, it is for the county of the trailer owner's residence.

STATE	FEE	LICENSES Issuing Office	SPEED LIMITS Day	Night
ALABAMA	(none required)	————	60 m.p.h.	50 m.p.h.
ALASKA	$4	Dept. of Revenue, Motor Vehicle Div., Juneau	50 m.p.h.	50 m.p.h.
ARIZONA	$6.25	Highway Dept., Motor Vehicle Div., Phoenix	65 m.p.h.	50 m.p.h.
ARKANSAS	$4.50 to 1,000 lbs. gross for 2-wheel trailers; all others $10	Revenue Dept., Motor Vehicle Div., Little Rock	60 m.p.h.	60 m.p.h.
CALIFORNIA	$11 plus 2% of value as assessed by Dept. of Motor Vehicles	Dept. of Motor Vehicles at Sacramento or any field office	55 m.p.h.	55 m.p.h.
COLORADO	$3-7.50	County clerk	reasonable and prudent	
CONNECTICUT	$3	Motor Vehicle Dept., Hartford	reasonable and proper	
DELAWARE	$2 per 500 lbs. to 5,000 lbs.; $2.60 per 500 lbs. over 5,000 lbs.	Motor Vehicle Div., Dover	55 m.p.h.	55 m.p.h.
DISTRICT of COLUMBIA	$8-32	Dept. of Motor Vehicles, Washington	25 m.p.h.	25 m.p.h.
FLORIDA	$5 to 500 lbs.; $2.50 plus 75¢ per 100 lbs. over 500 lbs. to 4,000 lbs.	Motor Vehicle Dept., Tallahassee	60 m.p.h.	55 m.p.h.
GEORGIA	$10	Dept. of Revenue, Motor Vehicle License Unit, Atlanta	60 m.p.h.	50 m.p.h.
HAWAII	load weight tax	Finance Dept., County of residence	45 m.p.h.	45 m.p.h.
IDAHO	$2.50-8	County assessor's office	70 m.p.h.	70 m.p.h.
ILLINOIS	$6-20	Office of Sec. of State, Auto Dept., Springfield	55 m.p.h.	55 m.p.h.
INDIANA	$3-8	Bureau of Motor Vehicles, Indianapolis	65 m.p.h.	65 m.p.h.
IOWA	$3-10	County treasurer's office	55 m.p.h.	55 m.p.h.
KANSAS	$5-10	County treasurer's office	70 m.p.h.	60 m.p.h.
KENTUCKY	none required	————	60 m.p.h.	50 m.p.h.
LOUISIANA	$3-20	Dept. of Revenue, Baton Rouge	60 m.p.h.	60 m.p.h.
MAINE	$2-5	Office of Sec. of State, Motor Vehicle Div., Augusta	45 m.p.h.	45 m.p.h.

STATE	FEE	LICENSES Issuing Office	SPEED LIMITS Day	Night
MARYLAND	$10-40	Dept. of Motor Vehicles, Baltimore	50 m.p.h.	50 m.p.h.
MASSACHUSETTS	$5 per 1,000 lbs. or fraction thereof of weight of trailer and maximum load	Div. of Registry of Motor Vehicles, Boston	50 m.p.h.	50 m.p.h.
MICHIGAN	$.55 per 100 lbs. to 1,000 lbs.; $1.40 per 100 lbs. from 1,000 lbs. to 6,000 lbs.	Office of Sec. of State, Div. of Driver and Vehicle Service, Lansing	65 m.p.h.	55 m.p.h.
MINNESOTA	$2.35 base	Office of Sec. of State, Motor Vehicle Div., St. Paul	60 m.p.h.	50 m.p.h.
MISSISSIPPI	$3.75	County sheriff's office	65 m.p.h.	65 m.p.h.
MISSOURI	$7	Dept. of Revenue, Motor Vehicle Reg., Jefferson City	70 m.p.h.	65 m.p.h.
MONTANA	$2 to 2,500 lbs. gross vehicle weight; $5, 2,500 lbs. to 6,000 lbs.; $10, over 6,000 lbs.	County treasurer's office	reasonable and proper	
NEBRASKA	$1 per 1,000 lbs.	Dept. of Roads and Irrigation, Motor Vehicle Div., Lincoln	50 m.p.h.	50 m.p.h.
NEVADA	$2.50 to 1,000 lbs. empty; $5.50, 1,001 to 3,500 lbs.; $8, 3,501 to 3,549 lbs. + privilege tax	Dept. of Motor Vehicles, Carson City	reasonable and proper	
NEW HAMPSHIRE	$2 base	Div. of Motor Vehicles, Dept. of Safety, Concord	60 m.p.h.	60 m.p.h.
NEW JERSEY	$5-10	Dept. of Law and Public Safety, Div. of Motor Vehicles, Trenton	50 m.p.h.	50 m.p.h.
NEW MEXICO	$5 plus $1 per 100 lbs. or fraction thereof in excess of 500 lbs.	Dept. of Motor Vehicles, Santa Fe	70 m.p.h.	50 m.p.h.
NEW YORK	$2.50 per 500 lbs.	Dept. of Motor Vehicles, Albany	50 m.p.h.	50 m.p.h.
NORTH CAROLINA	$3	Dept. of Motor Vehicles, Raleigh	55 m.p.h.	55 m.p.h.
NORTH DAKOTA	none required	————	65 m.p.h.	55 m.p.h.
OHIO	$.85 per 100 lbs. to 2,000 lbs.; $1.40 per 100 lbs., 2,000 lbs. to 3,000 lbs.; $1.90 per 100 lbs., 3,000 lbs. to 4,000 lbs.	Bureau of Motor Vehicles, Columbus	50 m.p.h.	50 m.p.h.

STATE	FEE	LICENSES Issuing Office	SPEED LIMITS Day	Night
OKLAHOMA	none required	————	50 m.p.h.	50 m.p.h.
OREGON	$10	Dept. of Transportation, Motor Vehicle Division, Salem	55 m.p.h.	55 m.p.h.
PENNSYLVANIA	$12	Dept. of Revenue, Bureau of Motor Vehicles, Harrisburg	50 m.p.h.	50 m.p.h.
RHODE ISLAND	$.15 per 100 lbs. gross wt. or fraction thereof	Registry of Motor Vehicles, Providence	reasonable and proper	
SOUTH CAROLINA	$7	Highway Dept., Motor Vehicle Div., Columbia	60 m.p.h.	55 m.p.h.
SOUTH DAKOTA	$2-15	County treasurer's office	50 m.p.h.	60 m.p.h.
TENNESSEE	none required	————	65 m.p.h.	55 m.p.h.
TEXAS	$.33 per 100 lbs. to 6,000 lbs. gross weight; $.44 per 100 lbs., 6,001 lbs. to 8,000 lbs.	County tax collector	60 m.p.h.	55 m.p.h.
UTAH	$5	Dept. of Motor Vehicles, Salt Lake City	70 m.p.h.	70 m.p.h.
VERMONT	$7.50-15	Dept. of Motor Vehicles, Montpelier	50 m.p.h.	50 m.p.h.
VIRGINIA	$6.50-12	Div. of Motor Vehicles, Richmond	65 m.p.h.	65 m.p.h.
WASHINGTON	$3.25-29.40	Secretary of State, Olympia	60 m.p.h.	60 m.p.h.
WEST VIRGINIA	$6-17	Dept. of Motor Vehicles, Charleston	55 m.p.h.	55 m.p.h.
WISCONSIN	$12.50	Motor Vehicle Dept., Madison	65 m.p.h.	55 m.p.h.
WYOMING	$1 to 1,000 lbs. empty; $7.50, 1,001 to 3,500 lbs.; $10, 3,501 to 4,500 lbs.	County treasurer's office	75 m.p.h.	65 m.p.h.

B. Trailer Fittings

The following list of trailer accessory manufacturers is based upon material that has appeared in *Boating Industry* magazine.

BALLS

Acme Products Co., Inc., 7300 E. 17th St., Kansas City, Mo. 64126.
Atwood Vacuum Machine Co., 1400 Eddy Ave., Rockford, Ill. 61101.
Certified Marine Industries, Div. Instrument Systems Corp., 7535 W. Fourth Ave., Hialeah, Fla. 33014.
Hammerblow Co., Div. LSI, 1000 First St., Wausau, Wis. 54401.
Nicson Engineering Co., 11850 Burke St., Santa Fe Springs, Calif.
Valley Tow-Rite Div., Scott & Fetzer Co., 27 E. Vine St., P.O. Box 850, Lodi, Calif. 95240.

BRAKES

Atwood Vacuum Machine Co., 1400 Eddy Ave., Rockford, Ill. 61101.
Balko, Inc., Box 168, Ladysmith, Wis. 54848.
Bendix Corp., Automotive Service Div., 1217 S. Walnut St., South Bend, Ind. 46620.
Boyer Industries, 460 W. 12th St., Erie, Pa. 16501.
Certified Marine Industries, Div. Instrument Systems Corp., 7535 W. Fourth Ave., Hialeah, Fla. 33014.
Dico Co., 20 S.W. 16th St., Des Moines, Iowa 50305.
Hadco Engineering Div., A-T-O Inc., 2000 Camfield Ave., Los Angeles, Calif. 90040.
Hammerblow Co., Div. LSI, 1000 First St., Wausau, Wis. 54401.
Holsclaw Bros., Inc., Box 4128, Station A, Evansville, Ind. 47711.
Hydro-Act Div., Toledo Stamping & Mfg. Co., Box 596, Toledo, Ohio
Industrial Fasteners Ltd. of No. America, 1510 McCormick Ave., Mundelein, Ill. 60060.
Kelsey Axle Div./Kelsey Hayes Co., 2825 Middlebury St., Elkhart, Ind. 46514.
Kelsey Hayes Co., Kelsey Products Div., 38481 Huron River Dr., Romulus, Mich. 48174.
Mercury Clutch Div., Automatic Steel Products, Inc., 1201 Camden Ave., Canton, Ohio 44706.
Nicson Engineering Co., 11850 Burke St., Santa Fe Springs, Calif.
Snow Corp., 4350 McKinley St., Omaha, Neb. 68112.
Stromberg Hydraulic Brake and Coupling Co., 5453 Northwest Hwy., Chicago, Ill. 60600.
Thorobred Trailers Div., Moore Corp., 653 New Circle Rd., Lexington, Ky. 40501.

COUPLERS

Acme Products Co., Inc., 7300 E. 17th St., Kansas City, Mo. 64126.
Atwood Vacuum Machine Co., 1400 Eddy Ave., Rockford, Ill. 61101.
Certified Marine Industries, Div. Instrument Systems Corp., 7535 W. Fourth Ave., Hialeah, Fla. 33014.

Dico Co., 200 S.W. 16th St., Des Moines, Iowa 50305.
Durbin-Durco, Inc., 1436 Woodson Rd., St. Louis, Mo. 63132.
Dutton-Lainson Co., 1601 W. Second St., Box 729, Hastings, Neb.
Fulton Co., 1912 S. 82nd St., Milwaukee, Wis. 53219.
Hammerblow Co., Div. LSI, 1000 First St., Wausau, Wis. 54401.
Marvel Industries, Inc., P.O. Box 388, Sturgis, Mich. 49091.
Nicson Engineering Co., 11850 Burke St., Santa Fe Springs, Calif.
Valley Tow-Rite Div., Scott and Fetzer Co., 27 E. Vine St., P.O. Box
    850, Lodi, Calif. 95240.

CRADLE PADS

Bud Enterprises, Inc., 2316 W. Brandon Blvd., Brandon, Fla. 33511.
Certified Marine Industries, Div. Instrument Systems Corp., 7535 W.
    Fourth Ave., Hialeah, Fla. 33014.
Fleet Cap'n Trailers, George Street, New Bern, N. C. 28560.
The Standard Products Co., Inc., 2130 W. 110th St., Cleveland, Ohio

DOLLIES

Alloy Marine, Inc., 4618 Point Tramble Rd., Algonac, Mich. 48001.
Boyer Industries, 460 W. 12th St., Erie, Pa. 16501.
Certified Marine Industries, Div. Instrument Systems Corp., 7535 W.
    Fourth Ave., Hialeah, Fla. 33014.
Dico Co., 200 S.W. 16th St., Des Moines, Iowa 50305.
Fleet Cap'n Trailers, George Street, New Bern, N. C. 28560.
Holsclaw Bros., Inc., Box 4128, Station A, Evansville, Ind. 47711.
International Erectors & Fabricators, Inc., P.O. Box 33, 360 Eastern
    Ave., Malden, Mass. 02148.
Lindy Marine Co., Div. Fecor Ind. Ltd., 99 Engineers Dr., Hicks-
    ville, N.Y. 11801.
Mastercraft Trailers Div., Bryan Metal Prod., Middlefield Street,
    Middletown, Conn. 06457.
Moto-Mover Div., M. K. Shields Co., 18632 Gault St., Reseda, Calif.
Simek Mfg. Inc., Shipmate Div., Townsend Avenue, Johnstown, N.Y.
Snow Corp., 4350 McKinley St., Omaha, Neb. 68112.
Tee-Nee Trailer Co., 215 E. Indianola Ave., Youngstown, Ohio 44507.
Williams Mfg. Co., P.O. Box 23, Wyncote, Pa. 19095.

HITCHES

Acme Products Co., Inc., 7300 E. 17th St., Kansas City, Mo. 64126.
Big Boy Products, Inc., P.O. Box 223, Warsaw, Ind. 46580.
Bock Ind., Inc., 2704 S. Napanee, Elkhart, Ind. 46514.
Boyer Industries, 460 W. 12th St., Erie, Pa. 16501.
Certified Marine Industries, Div. Instrument Systems Corp., 7535 W.
    Fourth Ave., Hialeah, Fla. 33014.
Draw-Tite Co., 14857 Martinsville, Belleville, Mich. 48111.
Durbin-Durco, Inc., 1435 Woodson Rd., St. Louis, Mo. 63132.
Fulton Co., 1912 S. 82nd St., Milwaukee, Wis. 53219.
Hadco Engineering Div., A-T-O Inc., 2000 Camfield Ave., Los
    Angeles, Calif. 90040.
Ideal Mfg. Co., 1107 S. Seventh St., Oskaloosa, Iowa 52577.
Magic Tilt Trailers, 2161 Lions Club Rd., Clearwater, Fla. 33516.
Nicson Engineering Co., 11850 Burke St., Santa Fe Springs, Calif.
Reese Products, 4013 Cassopolis Rd., P.O. Box 940, Elkhart, Ind.

Valley Tow-Rite Div., Scott & Fetzer Co., 27 E. Vine St., P.O. Box 850, Lodi, Calif. 95240.

HUB SEALERS AND PROTECTORS

Ace Welding and Trailer Works, 10235 Prospect Ave., Santee, Calif.

Aquappliances, Inc., 134 Bouquet Dr., San Marcos, Calif. 92069.

Certified Marine Industries, Div. Instrument Systems Corp., 7535 W. Fourth Ave., Hialeah, Fla. 33014.

Design Wheel and Hub, 2225 Lee Rd., Akron, Ohio 44306.

International Erectors and Fabricators, Inc., Box 33, 360 Eastern Ave., Malden, Mass. 02148.

Nicson Engineering Co., 11850 Burke St., Santa Fe Springs, Calif.

Noramgrex Co., P.O. Box 33, Malden, Mass. 02148.

Superior Sports Specialties, 558 Library St., San Fernando, Calif.

Wesbar Corp., Box 577, West Bend, Wis. 53095.

JACKS

Atwood Vacuum Machine Co., 1400 Eddy Ave., Rockford, Ill. 61101.

Bock Industries, Inc., 2704 S. Nappanee, Elkhart, Ind. 46514.

C and F Machine Works, 275 E. Marie, W. St. Paul, Minn. 55118.

Central Specialties Co., 6030 N. Northwest Hwy., Chicago, Ill. 60631.

Certified Marine Industries, Div. Instrument Systems Corp., 7535 W. Fourth Ave., Hialeah, Fla. 33014.

Conlan-Sieloff Industries, 3074 Rochester Rd., Troy, Mich. 48084.

Dico Co., 200 S.W. 16th St., Des Moines, Iowa 50305.

Fulton Co., 1912 S. 82nd St., Milwaukee, Wis. 53219.

Gill-Baum Mfg. Co., 1750 Summit St., New Haven, Ind. 46774.

Hammerblow Co., Div. LSI, 1000 First St., Wausau, Wis. 54401.

Holsclaw Bros., Inc., Box 4128 Station A, Evansville, Ind. 47711.

Marvel Ind., Inc., Box 327, Sturgis, Mich. 49091.

Mastercraft Trailers Div., Bryan Metal Prod., Middlefield Street, Middletown, Conn. 06457.

Snow Corp., 4350 McKinley St., Omaha, Neb. 68112.

Tide Craft, Inc., 1616 Shreveport Rd., P.O. Box 796, Minden, La.

LIGHTING KITS

Allan Marine, 91 Industry Court, Deer Park, N.Y. 11729.

American Trailer and Mfg. Co., 12222 S. Woodruff Ave., Downey, Calif. 90241.

Anderson Marine Div., Armacost Products Co., 4900 Blue Pkwy., Kansas City, Mo. 64130.

Armacost Products Co., 4900 Blue Pkwy., Kansas City, Mo. 64130.

Betts Machine Co., 1800 Pennsylvania Ave., P.O. Box 888, Warren, Pa. 16365.

Certified Marine Industries, Div. Instrument Systems Corp., 7535 W. Fourth Ave., Hialeah, Fla. 33014.

Cole-Hersee Co., 20 Old Colony Ave., Boston, Mass. 02727.

Do-Ray Lamp Co., Inc., 1468 S. Michigan Ave., Chicago, Ill. 60605.

Grote Mfg. Co., P.O. Box 766, Madison, Ind. 47250.

Holsclaw Bros., Inc., Box 4128 Station A, Evansville, Ind. 47711.

Mastercraft Trailers Div., Bryan Metal Prod., Middlefield Street, Middletown, Conn. 06457.

Miro-Flex Co., Inc., 3050 N. St. Francis, Wichita, Kans. 67219.

Nicson Engineering Co., 11850 Burke St., Santa Fe Springs, Calif.
Olson Industries, Inc., P.O. Box 2520, Sarasota, Fla. 33578.
Pathfinder Co., Div. Allen Electric & Equipment Co., 5445 N. Elston Ave., Chicago, Ill. 60630.
Richmond Marine Ltd., 48 The Green, Twickenham, Middlesex, England.
Simek Mfg. Inc., Shipmate Div., Townsend Avenue, Johnstown, N.Y.
J. W. Speaker Corp., 3059 N. Weil St., Milwaukee, Wis. 53212.
T and T Mfg. Co., 1115 Sixth St., Rockford, Ill. 61108.
Tee-Nee Trailer Co., 215 E. Indianola Ave., Youngstown, Ohio 44507.

LIGHTS

Allan Marine, 91 Industry Court, Deer Park, N.Y. 11729.
Anderson Marine Div., Armacost Products Co., 4900 Blue Pkwy., Kansas City, Mo. 64130.
Theodore Bargman Co., 13950 John R., Detroit, Mich. 48203.
Betts Machine Co., 1800 Pennsylvania Ave., P.O. Box 888, Warren, Pa. 16365.
Cats-Eye Lamp Div., 1341 Norton Ave., Columbus, Ohio 43212.
Certified Marine Industries, Div. Instrument Systems Corp., 7535 W. Fourth Ave., Hialeah, Fla. 33014.
R. E. Dietz Co., 225 Wilkinson St., Syracuse, N.Y. 13201.
Do-Ray Lamp Co., Inc., 1468 S. Michigan Ave., Chicago, Ill. 60605.
Groendyk Mfg. Co., Inc., P.O. Box 278, Buchanan, Va. 24066.
Grote Mfg. Co., P.O. Box 766, Madison, Ind. 47250.
Miro-Flex Co., Inc., 3050 N. St. Francis, Wichita, Kans. 67219.
Nicson Engineering Co., 11850 Burke St., Santa Fe Springs, Calif.
Olson Industries, Inc., P.O. Box 2520, Sarasota, Fla. 33578.
Pathfinder Co., Div. Allen Electric and Equipment Co., 5445 N. Elston Ave., Chicago, Ill. 60630.
Quaker State Oil Refining Corp., 11 Center St., Oil City, Pa. 16301.
Seminole Trailer Mfg. Corp., 895 W. 19th St., Hialeah, Fla. 33010.
J. W. Speaker Corp., 3059 N. Weil St., Milwaukee, Wis. 53212.

LOADING GUIDES

Certified Marine Industries, Div. Instrument Systems Corp., 7535 W. Fourth Ave., Hialeah, Fla. 33014.
Fleet Cap'n Trailers, George Street, New Bern, N.C. 28560.
Holsclaw Bros., Inc., Box 4128 Station A, Evansville, Ind. 47711.
Pipestone Marine Corp., Box 311, S. Highway 75, Pipestone, Minn.

OUTBOARD MOTOR BRACKETS

Langford Canoe Co., Rural Route 1, Baysville, Ont., Canada.

ROLLERS

American Trailer and Mfg. Co., 12222 S. Woodruff Ave., Downey, Calif. 90241.
Certified Marine Industries, Div. Instrument Systems Corp., 7535 W. Fourth Ave., Hialeah, Fla. 33014.
Dico Co., 200 S.W. 16th St., Des Moines, Iowa 50305.
Groendyk Mfg. Co., Inc., P.O. Box 278, Milwaukee, Wis. 53214.
Holsclaw Bros., Inc., Box 4128, Station A, Evansville, Ind. 47711.
Lake Rubber, Inc., Box 547, Willoughby, Ohio 44094.
Marine Rubber Products Co., Box 547, Willoughby, Ohio 44094.

Mastercraft Trailers Div., Bryan Metal Prod., Middlefield Street, Middletown, Conn. 06457.

Minisink Rubber Co., Inc., Orange County, Unionville, N.Y. 10988.

Moeller Mfg. Co., Inc., P.O. Box 1318, Greenville, Miss. 38701.

Neilson Wheel Co., 8301 W. Lapham St., Milwaukee, Wis. 53214.

The Ohio Rubber Co., Ben Hur Avenue, Willoughby, Ohio 44094.

Simek Mfg. Inc., Shipmate Div., Townsend Avenue, Johnstown, N.Y.

Wefco Rubber Mfg. Corp., 1655 Euclid St., Santa Monica, Calif.

SAFETY CHAINS

Acco (American Chain & Cable Co., Inc.), 929 Conn Ave., Bridgeport, Conn. 06602.

Big Boy Products Inc., P.O. Box 223, Warsaw, Ind. 46580.

Dade Trading Corp., 2425 N.W. 33rd Ave., Miami, Fla. 33142.

Dico Co., 200 S.W. 16th St., Des Moines, Iowa 50305.

Dixie Craft Trailers, Inc., P.O. Box 351, Europa, Miss. 39744.

Dutton-Lainson Co., 1601 W. Second St., P.O. Box 729, Hastings, Nebr. 68901.

Fulton Co., 1912 S. 82nd St., Milwaukee, Wis. 53219.

Ideal Mfg. Co., 1107 S. Seventh St., Oskaloosa, Iowa 52577.

Mastercraft Trailers Corp., Middlefield Street, Middletown, Conn.

Nicson Engineering Co., 11850 Burke St., Santa Fe Springs, Calif.

T and T Mfg. Co., 1115 Sixth St., Rockford, Ill. 61108.

Valley Tow-Rite Div., Scott & Fetzer Co., 27 E. Vine St., P.O. Box 850, Lodi, Calif. 95240.

SHOCK ABSORBERS

Armstrong Beverley Engineering Ltd., 4001 Cote Verte Rd., Montreal 383, Quebec, Canada.

Lord Mfg. Co., Div. Lord Corp., 1635 W. 12th St., Erie, Pa. 16512.

Monroe Auto Equipment Co., 1426 E. First, Monroe, Mich. 48161.

Texaco, Inc., 135 E. 42nd St., New York, N.Y. 10017.

United Motors Service Div., General Motors, 3044 West Grand Blvd., Detroit, Mich. 48202.

SPRINGS

Big Boy Products, Inc., P.O. Box 223, Warsaw, Ind. 46580.

Certified Marine Industries, Div. Instrument Systems Corp., 7535 W. Fourth Ave., Hialeah, Fla. 33014.

Hadco Engineering Div., A-T-O Inc., 2000 Camfield Ave., Los Angeles, Calif. 90040.

Hammerblow Co., Div. LSI, 1000 First St., Wausau, Wis. 54401.

Holsclaw Bros., Inc., Box 4128, Station A., Evansville, Ind. 47711.

International Spring Mfg. Co., 1510 McCormick Ave., Mundelein, Ill.

TIRES

Armstrong Rubber Co., Engineered Products Div., 1645 S. 83rd St., West Allis, Wis. 53214.

Certified Marine Industries, Div. Instrument Systems Corp., 7535 W. Fourth Ave., Hialeah, Fla. 33014.

The City Machine & Wheel Co., 1095 Home Ave., Akron, Ohio

Design Wheel & Hub, 2225 Lee Rd., Akron, Ohio 44306.

Dico Co., 200 S.W. 16th St., Des Moines, Iowa 50305.

Geneva Metal Wheel Co., Geneva, Ohio 44041.

Goodyear Tire & Rubber Co., Industrial Prod. Div., Akron, Ohio.
Mobiliner Tire Co., P.O. Box 497, Mansfield, Ohio 44901.
Neilson Wheel Co., 8301 W. Lapham St., Milwaukee, Wis. 53214.
Nicson Engineering Co., 11850 Burke St., Santa Fe Springs, Calif.
Seminole Trailer Mfg. Corp., 895 W. 19th St., Hialeah, Fla. 33010.
Snow Corp., 4350 McKinley St., Omaha, Nebr. 68112.
Trelleborg Rubber Co., Inc., 255 Main St., New Rochelle, N.Y. 10801.

WHEEL HUBS & BEARINGS
Ace Welding & Trailer Works, 10235 Prospect Ave., Santee, Calif.
Aquappliances, Inc., 134 Bouquet Dr., San Marcos, Calif. 92069.
Armstrong Rubber Co., Engineered Products Div., West Allis, Wis.
Certified Marine Industries, Div. Instrument Systems Corp., 7535 W.
     Fourth Ave., Hialeah, Fla. 33014.
City Machine & Wheel Co., 1095 Home Ave., Akron, Ohio 44310.
Design Wheel & Hub, 2225 Lee Rd., Akron, Ohio 44306.
Dico Co., 200 S. W. 16th St., Des Moines, Iowa 50305.
Dutton-Lainson Co., P.O. Box 729, Hastings, Nebr. 68901.
Geneva Metal Wheel, Geneva, Ohio 44041.
Hadco Engineering Div., A-T-O Inc., 2000 Camfield Ave., Los
     Angeles, Calif. 90040.
Hammerblow Co., Div. LSI, 1000 First St., Wausau, Wis. 54401.
Kelsey Axle Div./Kelsey Hayes Co., 2825 Middlebury St., Elkhart,
     Ind. 46514.
Kelsey Hayes Co., Kelsey Products Div., 38481 Huron River Dr.,
     Romulus, Mich. 48174.
Lincoln Foundry, 1510 McCormick Ave., Mundelein, Ill. 60060.
Neilson Wheel Co., 8301 W. Lapham St., Milwaukee, Wis. 53214.
Nicson Engineering Co., 11850 Burke St., Santa Fe Springs, Calif.
Noramgrex Co., P.O. Box 33, Malden, Mass. 02148.

WINCHES
American Gage and Mfg. Co., 550 W. Linfoot, Wauseon, Ohio 43567.
Balko Inc., Box 309, Ladysmith, Wis. 54848.
Big Boy Products, Inc., P.O. Box 223, Warsaw, Ind. 46580.
L.S. Brown Co., 228 Margaret St., S.E., Atlanta, Ga. 30315.
Dixie Craft Trailers, Inc., Box 351, Europa, Miss. 39744.
Draw-Tite Co., 14857 Martinsville, Belleville, Mich. 48111.
Fulton Co., 1912 S. 82nd St., Milwaukee, Wis. 53219.
G & G Metals Fabricating, 2237 S. Trail, Venice, Fla. 33595.
Holsclaw Bros. Inc., Box 4128, Station A, Evansville, Ind. 47711.
Howard Engineering, Inc., 1206 Kishwaukee St., Rockford, Ill. 61110.
Ideal Mfg. Co., 1107 S. Seventh St., Oskaloosa, Iowa 52577.
Magic Tilt Trailers, 2161 Lions Club Rd., Clearwater, Fla. 33516.
Mastercraft Trailers Corp., Middlefield Street, Middletown, Conn.
Powerwinch Corp., 13 Garden St., Bridgeport, Conn. 06605.
Seminole Trailer Mfg. Corp., 805 W. 19th St., Hialeah, Fla. 33010.
Snow Corp., 4350 McKinley St., Omaha, Nebr. 68112.
Superwinch, Inc., 20 Winch Rd., Pomfret, Conn. 06258.
T and T Mfg. Co., 1115 Sixth St., Rockford, Ill. 61108.
Tee-Nee Trailer Co., 215 E. Indianola Ave., Youngstown, Ohio 44507.
Valley Tow-Rite Div., Scott and Fetzer Co., Lodi, Calif. 95240.